Reviews for *The Lost Story of the William & Mary*

'I loved the salty air of Gill Hoffs' book. A terrific, rollicking adventure that will stay long in the memory.'

Simon Garfield, author of *Timekeepers*, editor of
A Notable Woman: The Romantic Journals of Jean Lucey Pratt

'Gill Hoffs has woven a story that is absorbing, well researched, and reads like a good adventure novel, only it's true. If you like reading tales of the sea, I can highly recommend this book!'

Deborah Patterson, Museum Curator,
***Wyannie Malone Historical Museum*, Hope Town, Abaco, Bahamas**

'The story is a pure sensory smorgasbord of life and death aboard an emigrant ship, complete with a cowardly, treacherous captain and crew, who leave the emigrants to die on a sinking ship.'

Dr Cathryn Pearce, author of
Cornish Wrecking, 1700–1860

'Gill Hoffs has written a thrilling account of a shipwreck and the experience of emigrants, using the words of the actors to tell their own story. But she does not neglect the wider context and picture of conditions at sea which makes this more than just the well-told story of a shipwreck, but a vignette of the perils facing men and women from nineteenth-century Europe in search of a better life overseas.'

Kevin Brown, author of *Passage to the World:*
The Emigrant Experience 1807–1940

'This is a masterfully written micro-history which uncovers an obscure, forgotten story of betrayal at sea, told in a fast-paced narrative that also illuminates the harsh realities of transatlantic migration in the Victorian era. Readers will find themselves quickly drawn into the story because of its compelling and real characters, but along the way will learn much about the world in which this crime occurred.'

Dr William Kerrigan, Cole Distinguished professor of
American History at Muskingum University

'*The Lost Story of the William and Mary* is an enthralling tale of an erstwhile time… What starts in historical sequence ends with a psychological interrogation of the human actors as the reader is witness to the wanton and the heroic, the reckless and the desperate, the doomed and the absconded.'

John H. Bickford III, Ph.D., Associate Professor of
Social Studies/History Education, Eastern Illinois University

Praise for Gill Hoffs' previous book, *The Sinking of RMS Tayleur: The Lost Story of the 'Victorian Titanic'* (2014, 2015) – also available from Pen & Sword

'… a gripping new book, *The Sinking Of RMS* Tayleur by Gill Hoffs, vividly tells the story of the *Tayleur*'s demise and reveals a compelling theory behind what caused this supposedly 'perfect' ship to sink.'

Daily Mail

'Book of the Month – A well-written and thoroughly researched account of this lesser-known tragedy.'

Sea Breezes Magazine

'A fascinating, well researched account of this memorable shipwreck … Highly recommended.'

Richard Larn OBE, author of
Lloyd's Shipwreck Index of Ireland and Great Britain

'… a rare and unusual find … heartbreaking and humbling.'

Joe Jackson, author of *Atlantic Fever*

'A first class voyage of discovery … a detailed and vivid account of the shameful loss of the *Tayleur* … in this skilful post-mortem of Victorian sea-going values.'

Dr Ronnie Scott, Centre for Open Studies,
University of Glasgow

'Gill Hoffs has given us a compelling, heart-rending read … RMS *Tayleur* is lost no more.'

Gregory Gibson, author of *Demon of the Waters*

'Gill Hoffs' maiden voyage as a major nautical-historical author comes off wonderfully … a vivid and frightening elegy.'

Marc Songini, author of *The Lost Fleet*

The Lost Story of the
William and Mary

For all those, then and now,
who risk their all in search of a better or longer life,
and all those who risk their all to help them.

Also Dick Francis and Richard Laymon,
who provided me with the escape I needed as a teenager,
and the authors, actors and artists who continue to do so now.

The Lost Story of the
William and Mary

The Cowardice of Captain Stinson

Gill Hoffs

PEN & SWORD
HISTORY

First published in Great Britain in 2016 by
Pen & Sword History
an imprint of
Pen & Sword Books Ltd
47 Church Street
Barnsley
South Yorkshire
S70 2AS

Copyright © Gill Hoffs 2016

ISBN 978 1 47385 824 4

A CIP catalogue record for this book is available from the British
Library

Typeset in Ehrhardt by
Mac Style Ltd, Bridlington, East Yorkshire
Printed and bound in the UK by CPI Group (UK) Ltd,
Croydon, CR0 4YY

Pen & Sword Books Ltd incorporates the imprints of Pen & Sword
Archaeology, Atlas, Aviation, Battleground, Discovery, Family
History, History, Maritime, Military, Naval, Politics, Railways, Select,
Transport, True Crime, and Fiction, Frontline Books, Leo Cooper,
Praetorian Press, Seaforth Publishing and Wharncliffe.

For a complete list of Pen & Sword titles please contact
PEN & SWORD BOOKS LIMITED
47 Church Street, Barnsley, South Yorkshire, S70 2AS, England
E-mail: enquiries@pen-and-sword.co.uk
Website: www.pen-and-sword.co.uk

Contents

List of Plates

A Court for King Cholera. (Punch, *25 September 1852*)

Father Thames introducing his offspring to the fair city of London. (Punch, *3 July 1853*)

Interior of a Cottage in the Isle of Skye. (Illustrated London News, *1853*)

Irish Emigrants Leaving Home – The Priest's Blessing. (Illustrated London News, *10 May 1851*)

Advertisement for the sailing of the *William and Mary*. (Liverpool Mercury, *15 March 1853. Image © THE BRITISH LIBRARY BOARD. ALL RIGHTS RESERVED. Image reproduced with kind permission of the British Newspaper Archive*)

Emigrants arrival at Cork – A Scene on the Quay. (Illustrated London News, *10 May 1851*)

Image of *William and Mary* from *Lotgevallen van den heer O. H. Bonnema*, 1853, used with kind permission of Collectie Tresoar.

Cabin of "The Madagascar" and female emigrants. (Illustrated London News, *12 March 1853*)

Map showing the doomed vessel's route through the Bahamas from *Lotgevallen van den heer O. H. Bonnema*, 1853, used with kind permission of Collectie Tresoar.

View from Fort Fincastle, across Nassau and out to sea, from *The Isles of Summer* by C. Ives (1880). This view from high ground at the back of Nassau shows the magnificent houses and lush foliage of the island, (*The Isles of Summer* by C. Ives, 1880). (*Images used with kind permission of Pennymead.com*)

Johannes (John) Tuininga; Trijntje (Catherine Tuininga) Albers de Haan; Jan (John) Tuininga. (*All Tuininga images used with kind permission of Christopher Lindstrom*)

Sake Kooistra (Silas Coster)

Sjoerd (Bekins) Bekius. (*Both images used with kind permission of Ann Bekins*)

Beitske (Betsey) Gartner née Graafsma. (*Image used with kind permission of Joan McWhirter*)

Arjen Westerhuis; Hanne Westerhuis (Henry Westerhouse). (*All Westerhouse images used with kind permission of Kim Frank*)

High mortality in the 1850s. (Illustrated London News, *2 April 1853*)

'Emigrants are not to be compared to other persons;
they are an exception;
they are the most helpless people in the world.'

Samuel Sidney,
First Report from the Select Committee on Emigrant Ships,
B.P.P., 1854, Vol. 13

Preface

When reading about Victorian maritime disasters in old newspapers while conducting research for my book *The Sinking of RMS Tayleur: The Lost Story of the 'Victorian Titanic'* (Pen & Sword, 2014, 2015), one shipwreck stood out as particularly odd among the thousands reported. The *William and Mary* was an ordinary vessel with a common name, which set sail from Liverpool in early 1853 without any sort of fanfare or special treatment. Nothing distinguished the parties of Irish, Scottish, English, Dutch and German emigrants on board, nor the captain and crew, from any of the thousands of others leaving port that month. But within a few months the *William and Mary* would provoke outrage in newspapers around the world.

The accounts I read at first bemoaned the loss of over 200 passengers and a handful of crew, hoped for the salvation of a group who might have made it onto a raft as the ship went down before the captain's eyes in the shark-infested waters of the Bahamas and hinted at their dissatisfaction with the captain and crew's 'hurry to yield to the instinct [of self-preservation]' (*Freeman's Journal*, 31 May 1853). Then, according to articles published just a few weeks later, the truth came out – or, at least, a version of it.

Captain Timothy Stinson, a self-assured American and the son-in-law of one of the owners of the ship, had slowly sailed his newly-built barque across the Atlantic towards its destination of New Orleans. Fourteen passengers died en route, perhaps hastened along by the lack of a ship's surgeon and Captain Stinson's prescription of (off) ham as a cure-all. Concerned by the cruelty of a crew who tortured the cook on deck and threatened the passengers with the same treatment if they complained, and frustrated by a lack of decent – or sometimes any – provisions, the emigrants worried about their possible starvation. They were overjoyed to see the land masses of the Bahamas on the horizon and celebrated with singing and dancing on deck. Unfortunately, the hazardous channel Stinson insisted on entering soon became the scene of disaster.

A storm tossed the *William and Mary* about, emptying emigrants from their bunks onto the deck and the ship was holed on first one rock then another, allowing water to gush into the hold. What happened next was brutal and bizarre and if it wasn't for the kindness of a local wrecker, the true story of Stinson and his crew's loathsome actions that could easily be interpreted as an attempt at mass murder would have been lost at sea along with over 200 passengers – which is probably just what Stinson hoped would happen.

I found the survivors' reports outrageous and infuriating, all the more so when I realised that Stinson and the worst of his crew got away with it. In a time where table-tapping was still reported to be a viable way of communicating with the spirit world and slaves were murdered as their owners saw fit in America, a time when values, knowledge and legalities were really quite alien to ours, I perhaps should not be as shocked as I am.

While this book focuses on the journey of the *William and Mary* across the Atlantic and the lives of the people connected with her short existence, the bravery and experiences of other emigrants and sailors, contemporary and historical, should also be considered. The sea – despite modern gadgetry, the coastguard and air-sea rescue services – is as perilous for the unwary and unlucky now as it was in the 1850s; kindness and bravery are still just as necessary and magical for those in need of heroes.

After so many lies and so many decades, it is impossible to say exactly what happened to whom in the chaos of the shipwreck. I have drawn from many contemporary news reports and survivor accounts as well as later articles and family histories and there are, as expected with any recounting of a traumatic event, many inconsistencies and contradictions. With the generous help and advice of many researchers, descendants and knowledgeable friends, I have attempted to get to the heart of the affair and allow the people involved to tell their own story wherever possible. Any and all mistakes are my responsibility alone.

I'm painfully aware that I cannot bring the dead to justice by writing about wretched rogues and angelic wreckers. But I can raise awareness of the victims' plight, a corrupt captain with blood on his conscience if not his actual hands and men trusted with the lives of hundreds who literally got away with murder.

This is their story and it deserves to be told.

Gill Hoffs
Warrington, 8 October 2015

Chapter One

America is to modern Europe ... the land of aspirations and dreams, the country of daring enterprise and the asylum of misfortune, which receives alike the exile and the adventurer, the discontented and the aspiring and promises to all a freer life and a fresher nature. The European emigrant might believe himself as one transported to a new world governed by new laws and finds himself at once raised in the scale of being – the pauper is maintained by his own labour, the hired labourer works on his own account and the tenant is changed into a proprietor, while the depressed vassal of the old continent becomes co-legislator and co-ruler, in a government where all power is from the people and in the people and for the people.

(Essay quoted in *Oxford Chronicle and Reading Gazette*, 23 October 1852)

Travelling to Liverpool, February–March 1853

Europe was a terrible place for the impoverished in 1853. For almost a decade people had suffered bad harvests and epidemics and the knock-on negative effects of populations adjusting and moving around in search of something better. Over a million had died in Ireland alone from the famine and accompanying pestilence that raged there for six years until 1851, leading at least a million more to emigrate and spread death and disease. As the *Galway Vindicator* said on 1 June 1853, 'The hell upon earth, which England has made in Ireland, is quite enough to drive any people into the Atlantic, even if there were no promised land beyond.'

The newspapers were full of hideous accounts of poverty, disease, murder and suicide and had been so for several years. Parents were reported to have eaten their dead babies out of sheer desperation, starting with their legs so as to avoid as far as possible the faces they once kissed. Stray dogs grew fat clearing corpses from the ditches and hovels where they lay unburied, sometimes biting the dying as well. A working Irishman would have ordinarily consumed up to 14lbs/6.5kgs of potatoes a day along with some buttermilk and seaweed or shellfish if he lived by the coast but, despite food still being exported from Ireland, many were reduced to gnawing leather and roots to survive.

A Captain Wynne, working in County Clare as part of the relief effort, said,

> ... although a man not easily moved, I confess myself unmanned by the extent and intensity of the suffering I witnessed, more especially amongst the women and little children, crowds of whom were to be seen scattered over the turnip fields, like a flock of famishing crows, devouring the raw turnips, mothers half naked, shivering in the snow and sleet, uttering exclamations of despair whilst their children were screaming with hunger; I am a match for anything else I may meet with here, but this I cannot stand ...

Although the blight that turned whole fields of potatoes to inedible black sludge for two years in a row had now passed, the resulting starvation and desperation crippled Ireland and the countries around her. As one American visitor said, 'There is nothing unnatural in the desire of the unfortunate Irish to abandon their cheerless and damp cottages and to crawl inch by inch, while they have yet a little strength, from the graves which apparently yawn for their bodies.' (Evidence of Hon. Dudley Mann, who wrote from Bremen to the Select Committee of the Senate of the United States on the Sickness and Mortality on Board Emigrant Ships, 1854, 33rd Congress, 1st Session, Senate Rep. Com. No. 286.) Unfortunately, they took their problems with them.

Jobs and accommodation in Scotland, England and Wales became ever scarcer. Working conditions and pay were appalling. If miners were crushed in a pitfall or blown to pieces in an explosion, or labourers and seamstresses dropped dead of exhaustion, there were always plenty more to take their place. The Irish were resented and often shunned, while at the same time their willingness to work for a lower wage or in demonstrably unsafe conditions was used to force local workers to accept changes for the worse. This wasn't something that either the incoming Irish or the local population were happy about. Many campaigned for better conditions or government-assisted schemes to enable those who wished to do so to emigrate, but politicians saw that thousands were already leaving the British Isles on a daily basis – with an estimated 369,000 leaving Ireland in 1852 alone – and saw no need to pay for something which was occurring anyway.

The people who left home, unless their passages were paid for by their landlord or a charitable institution, were generally well enough off to be able to scrape together the money to travel and sustain themselves on the journey, but not so prosperous as to be able to live at home in comfort. They were feeling the pinch but capable of changing their location – and, they hoped, their circumstances. As the *Freeman's Journal* of 8 April 1852 put it, 'If Europeans enjoyed liberty and prosperity at home, they would not abandon their natal soil, where lie the bones of their ancestors and brave the perils of the ocean to seek an asylum in a strange land.'

Some committed crimes in the hopes of being transported elsewhere as punishment, or at least being fed and housed albeit miserably in a prison or workhouse – some of which crammed people seventeen to a bed, instead of the more usual five or six. Others were more creative in their approach, like the labourers in Connaught who put 6d. each into a general fund on payday then drew tickets from a hat, the one with 'America' written on it entitling the bearer to passage on an emigrant ship along with a small sum of money to provide for him once he landed.

Those who left Europe for a new life or an escape from their old one generally fled to Australia, Canada or America. Australia was the furthest away and most expensive, while Canada was infamous for its harsh winters and even harsher immigration procedures, with many would-be immigrants wary of the lethal fever sheds and quarantine restrictions on Grosse Isle and other destinations. Many Irish also disliked the idea of settling in a British colony. The United States was comparatively close, cheap and welcoming.

It wasn't just the Irish who were 'infatuated with the demon for change', as the *Bath Chronicle and Weekly Gazette* put it on 2 June 1853. British families were frustrated with the class system and the efforts of those of a 'better' class to keep them in their 'place' and also with the lack of prospects for their children. The quality and availability of education was extremely variable and over 700 teachers in 1851 couldn't even sign their own names. One man in Herefordshire was asked his reasons for emigrating from 'a fertile spot …

in one of the finest parts of that beautiful county' and replied "I have cause enough for going; *here* I have no school for my children[1] ... *in America* I am told my children will be taught by the State and I can get as much for a day and a half's work as is now paid me for the week.'

Amid the crowded towns and cities where people slept in rooms and cellars alongside total strangers on floors cushioned in the worst dwellings only by their own faeces and vomit, the idea of America's fresh air and open space was immensely appealing. Dr Letheby, reporting on conditions for the poor to the Commissioners of Sewers for London a few years later in 1857, said,

> I have seen grown persons of both sexes sleeping in common with their parents, brothers and sisters and cousins and even the casual acquaintance of a day's tramp, occupying the same bed of filthy rags or straw; a woman suffering in travail, in the midst of males and females of different families that tenant the same room, where birth and death go hand in hand; where the child but newly born, the patient cast down with fever and the corpse waiting for interment, have no separation from each other, or from the rest of the inmates.... These rooms are ... wretchedly dirty and miserably furnished – in fact, they are infested with that peculiarly fusty and sickening smell which is characteristic of the filthy haunts of poverty. There also lurk the germs of disease which wait only for one last condition to bring them into frightful activity.

The clean rivers and lakes of the Americas would have been almost unimaginable for the likes of 22-year-old would-be emigrant Joseph Brooks and his wife, Mary Ann, in London. A few years earlier, Henry Mayhew wrote of a visit to one of the poorer areas in the capital, saying,

> ... the masses of filth and corruption round the metropolis are, as it were, the nauseous nests of plague and pestilence. Indeed, so well known are the localities of fever and disease, that London would almost admit of being mapped out pathologically and divided into its morbid

---

1. 'There was no school in that or the adjoining parish.' (*Hereford Times*, 1 January 1853).

districts and deadly cantons. We might lay our fingers on the Ordnance map and say here is the typhoid parish and there the ward of cholera; for as truly as the West-end rejoices in the title of Belgravia, might the southern shores of the Thames be christened Pestilentia ...

[T]he air has literally the smell of a graveyard and a feeling of nausea and heaviness comes over any one unaccustomed to imbibe the musty atmosphere. It is not only the nose, but the stomach, that tells how heavily the air is loaded with sulphuretted hydrogen; and as soon as you cross one of the crazy and rotting bridges over the reeking ditch, you know, as surely as if you had chemically tested it, by the black colour of what was once the white-lead paint upon the door-posts and window-sills, that the air is thickly charged with this deadly gas. The heavy bubbles which now and then rise up in the water show you whence at least a portion of the mephitic compound comes, while the open doorless privies that hang over the water side on one of the banks and the dark streaks of filth down the walls where the drains from each house discharge themselves into the ditch on the opposite side, tell you how the pollution of the ditch is supplied.

The water is covered with a scum almost like a cobweb and prismatic with grease. In it float large masses of green rotting weed and against the posts of the bridges are swollen carcasses of dead animals, almost bursting with the gases of putrefaction. Along its shores are heaps of indescribable filth, the phosphoretted smell from which tells you of the rotting fish there, while the oyster shells are like pieces of slate from their coating of mud and filth. In some parts the fluid is almost as red as blood from the colouring matter that pours into it from the reeking leather-dressers' close by.

This was where families bathed and emptied their buckets of night soil and left tubs of water to 'settle' in order to skim off the floating layer of effluent and impurities so they could have a drink. Compared to this hell on earth, a countryside where fruit was there for the taking, animals were there for the hunting and a fresh start was guaranteed, seemed like paradise and for many it was. For every word of warning to the intending emigrant there was another extolling the virtues of life abroad. But even amongst the most extravagant praise there were notes of caution reminding travellers of the need to work. A gardener from Aberdeen, now settled in New Jersey, wrote home,

To the labourer I would say, here is a wide field for you, plenty of employment and higher remuneration than at home; but do not, for a moment, imagine that labour is lighter, or that less will be required of you. No employer, or boss, as they are called here, will tolerate an indolent workman in his employment. The Americans in general are a most industrious and persevering people; they know how to value time. To the man with a rising family and possessing a small capital, wherewith he may purchase a piece of land, great encouragement is held forth … to one and all I would say, do not flatter yourselves with great prospects of success at first; no one ought to expect that in a strange country he will escape, in the first place, hardships and difficulties even greater than those at home. Many persons … have returned home, dispirited and disappointed, their money gone and their time lost, simply because they did not find America to be the fairy land of hoarded plenty they had expected …

The *Cork Examiner* of 30 March 1853 also spoke to would-be emigrants with money, saying, 'America presents to the large capitalist ample scope for enterprise and industry. Her wide extensive prairies and immense forests invite the scientific and wealthy agriculturist to settle within their bosom, each affording him abundant occupation suitable to his taste, either in clearing the lands of its ancient and stately possessors, or in adorning it with those plantations which beautify the scenery and impart grandeur to the view.' They were not alone in neglecting to mention the slaves and brutality associated with establishing and running plantations, nor the tribes who had lived in the prairies and forests for many centuries before white settlers started to lay claim to areas of land. Their assumption that emigrants reading the article would be people with means and money seems somewhat misguided, even by standards of the time.

That February in the Netherlands, however, aspirations were far grander and more organised than those of the families and individuals setting forth

from Ireland, England and Scotland for the prime port of Liverpool. Oepke
Bonnema, a philanthropic grain merchant described later in the press as 'a
young man of capital and energy' (e.g. *The Picayune, De Nieuwsbode*, 21 June
1853) had organised a settlement party in Friesland, a northern province
in the Netherlands, with the intention of establishing a town in the United
States. Ninety-one men, women and children arranged to travel with him
as a group, with Bonnema paying for their passage and provisions on the
understanding that they would work for their board and keep on arrival and
repay the costs at a rate of four guilders a week.

His plan was simple: sail from Harlingen in Friesland to Lowestoft in
Suffolk, the easternmost town in England, then travel by train to Liverpool
and board the steamship *Philadelphia*, bound for New Orleans. From there
they would travel by steamer up the Mississippi to their destination. But
when 27-year-old party member Hendrik Jans Kas later wrote, '… we have
experienced a great deal during our immigration …' it was an enormous
understatement. It seemed like nothing could go right for them.

Izaak Epkes Roorda, a 21-year-old painter and glasscutter, had heard a lot
about North America from neighbours who 'left for that country of hope
and expectation, in search of a new Fatherland', and he and others read of
life there in newspapers and books until 'it gradually awoke in me the desire
to make my own way to that country as soon as possible, in the supposition
that it would be easier for me there than in my Fatherland to achieve an
independent existence as a young man'. He thought he was more likely to
secure work there than in Friesland and since his brothers were already
trained in their father's trade, he didn't feel he was 'wholly necessary to my
parents for the exercise of their vocation'.

When he heard from some of his fellow villagers that Bonnema intended
to emigrate to the United States

with the aim of going deep inland to form a colony in the new state of
Iowa on the Missouri river, whence the Lord very gladly desired to lead a
certain number of fellows from our region, … [I] immediately expressed
to my parents this heartfelt wish of mine; to my delight they had no
great objection to this and following a long and mature deliberation,
on January 3rd this year, my Father consented to my request to write

to Mr Bonnema and set out the reasons that had brought me to ask to leave for America under his leadership and in his service, as well as the message that I was a housepainter by trade and not wholly unskilled in farming and gardening … [I] received an answer from Mr Bonnema himself, in which we were given to understand that should he perceive everything to conform to what we had written, he was inclined to agree to my request.

Roorda and his father soon met with Bonnema to discuss the possibility of Roorda joining the party, 'we quickly came to an agreement that I would enter into his service as a glassmaker and farmer for fl4.00 a week, with free food and accommodation, with him paying the travel costs from Harlingen to our destination, costs which I would gradually repay to him in America out of my earnings.'

His parents helped him prepare for the trip and he soon received a letter confirming the departure date, but there was trouble ahead.

As the shipping route was blocked and the ice was at the same time too weak to be used, while the sand roads were almost impassable because of the large amount of snow which had fell and the consequent long thaw, I had great difficulty in bringing my case to Leeuwarden, so that we eventually decided to take a goods wagon, while I left on foot, accompanied by two of my brothers and on Friday February 26th said farewell to my parents and other relatives.

Upon arriving in Leeuwarden, the capital city of Friesland, he loaded his belongings onto one of the wagons that took butter to Harlingen and rode 17 miles west to the port. 'It is difficult to describe the noise and bustle that existed at the harbour, both from the great number of people who like me were all set to leave the Fatherland under the leadership of Mr Bonnema and depart for another part of the world and from the loading of all their belongings onto the great English steamship the *City of Norwich* and the numerous acquaintances, relatives and onlookers who had gathered there to witness our departure from the harbour.'

The *City of Norwich* was one of several ships run by the North of Europe Steam Navigation Company and it regularly steamed between England and mainland Europe with livestock, passengers and cargo. According to an advert in the *London Daily News* on 2 February 1853, 'These favourite Steam-ships are elegantly fitted up for passengers and contain abundant stowage for goods.' But this wasn't what Bonnema and his group found. As Roorda later wrote, 'We were all under the impression that the boat would depart at 11 o'clock in the morning, by which many went into the city in the morning to carry out this or other errand, yet when at 8 o'clock Mr Bonnema was on board the ship and all goods were loaded on, the ropes were immediately loosened, notwithstanding that many of our company were missing. On hearing what was happening these people came running in great haste and were brought on board the steamship in two dinghies, with the exception of a girl and a young boy who were too late and had to stay behind, notwithstanding that their possessions were already on board the steamboat.' The two left behind wouldn't realise for several months that they had actually had a lucky escape.

Broer Baukes Haagsma, a 22-year-old teacher assisting Bonnema with the organisation of the trip, later recalled their departure from Harlingen at 9 am, saying,

The scene we witnessed there was heart-rending. Those tense moments between those hundreds of relatives and friends, in which people once more bade each their farewell and we left the soil of Friesland, we will never forget. I never hovered between hope and fear more than I did during those moments. Driven by a strong northeasterly wind the crowd soon vanished from our sight and only the coast of Friesland was visible. It was covered with snow and looked like a bank of chalk. As to the arrangements on the boat, they were far from what we might have desired.

As the group of ninety-two began their 150-mile voyage to Suffolk with ninety-nine oxen and 152 sheep sharing space on deck, they had an unpleasant surprise. As Roorda remembered it, 'as soon as we were out of the harbour, we saw quickly round about us where we could sit or lie, yet to this end we found nothing other than a little straw, which we left to the women and children and ourselves walked back and forth from one place to the other, because as there were no benches on board the ship and our cases were loaded beneath, we had no other place to sit than on the boards on the deck of the ship.' This might have proved no more than an unpleasant annoyance in better conditions. However,

[w]hile the weather was extremely unsettled, with terrible storms accompanied by heavy snowfalls, our uncomfortable situation was worsened for the most of us by the so dreadful seasickness, by which we on deck and crammed in among each other possessed neither the will nor the strength to change position and found it impossible to find any rest. The terrible weather made it necessary for the captain to drop anchor at 11 o'clock and when at 5 o'clock in the evening, when the storm had calmed somewhat, it was raised again we could still see Harlingen. Yet the ship quickly rocked again, so that we were unable to reach the Nieuwe Diep before 8 o'clock the following morning, where a great number of cattle and sheep were loaded on to the steamship, which did not improve our situation, as we found ourselves and the animals together in one section.

As soon as this cargo was on board, we set steam immediately for the North Sea and left for good the coast of our Fatherland, yet we had hardly been four hours at sea when another severe storm blew up, which lasted for the whole of the day and the following night; the ship swayed so violently that notwithstanding that the fences holding back the animals were four feet high, many cows were thrown over these and we had to continuously hold on to one or other part of the boat so that we were not thrown from one side to the other. Swept forward by the storm, the ship arrived the same evening at Lowestoft and we found ourselves, because of the darkness there, in the greatest danger of suffering a shipwreck on the English coast, yet luckily the machine was working, the ship moved back into deep water and a few hours later we steamed happily into the harbour of Lowestoft and found ourselves safe on the English quayside. Although it was in the depth of the night, 12 o'clock, the animals were immediately unloaded first, fed and watered straight away and driven thereafter onto the railway train to be transported to London.

The livestock was worth more than the human cargo and treated accordingly, both in person and in print. When the *Norfolk Chronicle* of 12 March 1853 reported the situation, there was no mention whatsoever of the emigrants or their suffering:

> The North of Europe Steam Navigation Company's steamer ship, *City of Norwich*, Thomas Forster Cockburn, commander, sailed from Harlingen on Saturday, laden with cattle and a general cargo. The weather being thick with snow she grounded on a mud bank. She was subsequently backed off and took the ground astern, doing serious damage to her rudder. This having been temporarily secured she proceeded to Nieu Dieppe and having taken in the remainder of her cargo, made for this port off which she arrived about noon; when about to enter the harbour, the rudder, from a sudden strain upon it, dropped off. She was afterwards assisted in by two steam tugs. It was a fortunate thing this serious occurrence did not take place at sea. She had on board 89 beasts, 18 sheep and three pigs, besides bacon, &c.

Bonnema had been advised against sailing in February: storms were likely to make any crossing a rough one and any emigrants travelling then would suffer with the cold, but he appears to have been quite a headstrong man and refused to alter his plans. His friend Haagsma clearly appreciated the seamanship of the steamer's young captain, praising his 'skilled management' and ability to guide the *City of Norwich* through the storm and into the harbour of Lowestoft 'after the bright beams of the moon had dispelled the darkness of night'.

The Frisians, along with the German and Irish emigrants they would soon meet in Liverpool, may have suffered discomfort on the open deck of their vessel, but they were probably safer there than below deck. Only a few years earlier under similar weather conditions, the *Londonderry* was the scene of 'a dreadful spectacle'. As *The Illustrated London News* reported on 9 December 1848:

[T]he steamer left Sligo for Liverpool on Friday evening, having onboard, besides cattle, nearly 150 passengers, the greater part of whom were on the way to America. The evening became so boisterous that none but the crew could keep the deck and the passengers were accordingly ordered below. The hatch, or companion, was drawn across but the space for ventilation being insufficient, the unfortunate people below were subjected to the horrible and lingering death of suffocation. One passenger, more fortunate than the rest, succeeded in gaining the deck and having alarmed the crew, an effort was made for their relief, but too late, 73 human beings having ceased to exist.

It took three hours and a half to get the dead out of the vessel and, as putrefaction had begun, the smell was so offensive that spirits were given to the men to keep them in a state of half-drunkenness to get them to go below. The place in which the poor creatures met their fate was about 20 feet long, 14 feet wide and 7 feet high. It had capacity for about 30 passengers but, so crowded was it, that the dead lay four deep on the floor.

There were some changes in legislation after this disaster, but not enough to make a positive difference to the human cargo in British waters. Although they were no longer allowed to be stuffed into small spaces without ventilation, passengers did not have an easy time of it on deck, as the Frisians had found out. Not everyone accepted this state of affairs, though and some people campaigned against such poor conditions. As the adventuring philanthropist Vere Foster wrote in 1852,

the cool indifference of the British government, on both sides of the [Irish] Channel, to the wholesale sufferings of the poor Irish emigrants of both sexes and of all ages … is truly lamentable … [One] cause of great suffering to emigrants [is] the want of shelter for deck passengers on board of steamers plying from Irish ports to Liverpool. While horses are most carefully protected on all sides and overhead from the inclemency of the weather, men, women and children are exposed, perfectly shelterless, in all seasons and in all weathers.

Haagsma, Bonnema and the other Frisians watched their chests and cases being offloaded from the steamer and talked to the port's customs officers. After that, Haagsma remembered that they 'found a warm room to stay in and warm coffee for our refreshment'. Then they boarded a train for their journey 230 miles west to Liverpool and left at 8 o'clock the next morning. Roorda later wrote he was

> greatly relieved that we were no longer on the ship where we had suffered so much and enjoyed no rest; for now we could go and sit and relax and although it was quite cold, this did not hinder us, as each of us wrapped around a blanket that Mr Bonnema had bought for us, without which we surely would have suffered much from the cold.
>
> We saw many new and strange things on this journey, though sadly we could only perceive a few things very fleetingly, owing to the great speed at which the train travelled. The way led through hills and valleys and among the things we saw along the way was a great number of steam factories varying greatly in construction, but we did not know what was made in all these places, we also noticed various [wind]mills built entirely of steel with five sails. When we first left Lowestoft the country was entirely covered in snow and we saw children walking on the ice, but gradually the countryside acquired a less wintry appearance, so that in the afternoon we began to see meadows with cows in them; these were all red and white and smaller than in Friesland; the country also looked to be less suitable for cultivation as it seemed to us to be very rocky, the farmers' houses we saw are smaller than those in the province of my birth; as we saw it men there left the hay on the land until winter before bringing it into storage, for we saw here and there a great deal of hay left outside.
>
> Along the way we passed through a few small tunnels and one large one, being a way beneath and straight through a hill, which was built entirely from stone, in which it at once became so dark that we could not see each other, this happened so suddenly and so unexpectedly that we did not know at first what was happening to us, yet just as abruptly we saw daylight again when we had passed through the tunnel. Shortly after we had been through this as it were underground way, we saw

on the road a very strange church building on which I could count 24 towers or spires.

The Frisians made an impression on the English, particularly when they had to take a break at the yellow-brick station of Ely to allow the cattle to change trains for London. 'We had to remain there until two thirty and meanwhile toured the city, to the great amusement of the residents. The wooden shoes and silver ear ornaments [traditional Frisian dress] caused people to stare at us,' recalled Haagsma, who was impressed with what he saw of England, saying 'at Peterborough ... they have a station 160 feet in length. The beautiful scene across hills and valleys, along woods and creeks soon disappeared. They were covered by the dark evening fog, which alas prevented the inquisitive traveller from seeing any more. But I know this, that we passed through tunnels three times, which are the result of the iron will of English enterprise.'

They reached Liverpool at around 5 am on Tuesday 1 March, as Roorda said

hoping to be able to depart again the following day with the steamship *Philadelphia*, yet very quickly we received the sad news that all passenger places on that boat were already taken, so that there was no opportunity for our company to leave for the New World by that option; we also heard that a sailing ship would leave on March 16th for New Orleans, which was equipped to carry as well as merchant goods a number of passengers. Mr Bonnema immediately made use of this opportunity through the generous mediation of Messrs. Vos and Brown and after quickly coming to an arrangement with the owners or the captain of the ship, it was now determined that we would leave for America in sixteen days' time with the barque *William and Mary*, commanded by Captain Stinson.

This would prove for many to be a fatal mistake.

Chapter Two

The huge steamer Great Britain, *bound for Australia, lies right off the Rock Ferry landing; and at a little distance are two old hulks of ships of war, dismantled, roofed over and anchored in the river, formerly for quarantine purposes, but now used chiefly or solely as homes for old seamen, whose light labor it is to take care of these condemned ships. There are a great many steamers plying up and down the river to various landings in the vicinity; and a good many steam-tugs; also, many boats, most of which have dark-red or tan-colored sails, being oiled to resist the wet; also, here and there, a yacht or pleasure-boat and a few ships riding stately at their anchors, probably on the point of sailing. The river, however, is by no means crowded; because the immense multitude of ships are ensconced in the docks, where their masts make an intricate forest for miles up and down the Liverpool shore. The small black steamers, whizzing industriously along, many of them crowded with passengers, snake up the chief life of the scene. The Mersey has the color of a mud-puddle and no atmospheric effect, as far as I have seen, ever gives it a more agreeable tinge.*

(Nathaniel Hawthorne, US Consul, 9 August 1853)

Preparing for the Voyage, Liverpool, February–March 1853

While Bonnema and the rest of the Frisian group travelled from their homes in the Netherlands for Liverpool and would-be emigrants in Britain and Ireland sold off or gave away any possessions they could do without or simply couldn't bring with them, the captain and crew of an unremarkable ship were settling into Liverpool and unloading their cargo. The *William and Mary* sailed from Charleston, South Carolina, on 4 January with a cargo of upland cotton for Liverpool, having completed her maiden voyage from Bath, Maine to Charleston with a load of hay and herring a short while before. A three-masted sailing ship of modest proportions, this was her first voyage across the Atlantic.

The ship entered the docks in Liverpool on 23 February, two days before Izaak Roorda took leave of his parents and began his journey to the ferry at Harlingen. Little of note occurred during the voyage and the occasional gale encountered at sea was endured without incident. At 137 feet long, the *William and Mary* was able to carry a load of up to 512 tons, which would require careful placement and securing within the hold to avoid the vessel heeling over at sea or incurring damage to the goods. Instead of returning to the Unites States with a ballast of bricks or coal, which cost money and would require loading and unloading, the ship was fitted out for the emigrant trade. Human cargo of this kind was ideal as emigrants and other travellers would actually pay to be taken aboard and load themselves – it was just their luggage and provisions that would need taken on. As the *Freeman's Journal* of 6 February 1852 commented, 'The overwhelming majority of the emigrants from the British Islands are Irish and by their conveyance to [America] shipowners have for years been realising large fortunes.'

The passengers booking berths on the *William and Mary* would have looked forward to better conditions on board if the ship had started off as an emigrant vessel in an American port. Two Acts of Congress there in 1847 (An Act to regulate the carriage of passengers in merchant vessels, February 22, 1847; and an amending act of March 2, 1847) required that in all emigrant ships each passenger should have fourteen or more square feet of deck space and to help prevent overcrowding the captain would be liable to a fine of $50 or one year in prison for each passenger they carried above the number allowed. The British regulations permitted no less than twelve feet to each passenger, unless they were travelling to the tropics, and whereas the American law considered each child – however young – as one full passenger, the British rules allowed two children under 14 to be calculated as only one statute passenger. This rule applied to the allocation of provisions too, so families would have far less food and water allotted to them under British rules than if they travelled on an American emigrant ship. Overall, British ships were allowed to carry half again as many passengers as an American vessel, when calculated on the ship's tonnage.

But with vast numbers of emigrants flocking to the docks daily, 'although there is a temporary falling off in the emigration to Australia, the exodus to America is now so brisk that difficulty is felt in procuring vessels to convey the new home-seekers from Liverpool' (*Stamford Mercury*, 3 June 1853) and Bonnema and his party had certainly found the popularity of their intended transport, the steamship *Philadelphia*, meant a change in their plans.

Liverpool was a busy port, welcoming shiploads of cotton, timber, molasses, rice, turpentine, cocoa, ginger, brimstone, coffee, cowhides, fustic, jute, palm oil, pepper, sugar, saltpetre, tallow, tobacco, tar and rum, and the most popular port for emigrants in Britain and Ireland, if not Europe as a whole, although it did not have the best reputation. The campaigner Vere Foster said in the *Wells Journal*, 15 May 1852, 'Vessels sail for America from Liverpool, London, Glasgow, Dublin, Cork, Limerick, Galway and London-derry. As regards mere ships, Liverpool ranks highest; as regards treatment of passengers, lowest.' Indeed, the *Limerick and Clare Examiner* of 24 July 1852 printed this plea to people considering a life abroad:

Few are they indeed who can witness without pain the manner in which Emigrants thither are treated and the shameful want of accommodation and over-crowding which attend them in most circumstances either in Liverpool or Glasgow. We have always been against the emigrant sailing from any but the nearest port. It is almost always the safest and must be uniformly a better and cheaper method of emigration. The emigrant, shipping at home, avoids all the expense of travel and the inconvenience of looking after stores and baggage and he escapes all traps of the man-catchers; and the plunder and villany [*sic*] of the slop-sellers which infest the great emporiums we have named. We would most earnestly impress it on all classes of our countrymen who mean to emigrate to make the point of their departure the nearest seaport to their old homes where they can have suitable accommodation.

Liverpool was also unpopular with sailors, as its rules prohibiting the use of lights and open flames on board moored vessels meant men wishing to cook their provisions, heat a drink or see their way to bed or below decks were unable to do so and had to request (and be granted) leave to spend their time and money on shore instead. This had its own dangers and one American captain said in a letter published in the *Morning Chronicle*, between 1849–51, 'Liverpool is notorious for the depravity of the population, male and female, that make it their business to prey upon the sailor … It used to be and I believe is still, the practice in Liverpool, to "skin" the sailors – that is for prostitutes to rob them of their clothes and send them out into the streets in a state of nudity.'

Another captain said in the same publication, 'All the captains that I know dread coming to Liverpool and would never come if they could help it … On arriving at Liverpool we generally lose two-thirds of our crew before we have been three days in port.' Stinson, however, retained his crew, probably benefitting from the ties most of them shared through being born or at least raised in the same area of Maine, rather than forcing them to remain on ship while in dock as some of the more desperate or tyrannical captains did.

Captain Timothy Reirdan Stinson, a 32-year-old, was described by Haagsma as 'a man with a fine seaman's appearance; but in his bearing there was something which I might properly call American pride which was apparent and often noticed in the seamen.' His father-in-law was part-owner of the ship, along with the ship's builder, John Harward and several others. It was common practice for captains to have an interest in the ship they mastered and he probably had a 1/16th share himself. Stinson grew up in Bowdoinham, Maine, where that ship and many others were built and there was a thriving coastal industry. A year later on 13 June 1854 the *Belfast Mercury* wrote, 'The State of Maine alone (it is said in the New York Shipping List) has added 11,000 tons to the merchant service since last May. Most of the merchant vessels built there have been of the first class – large clippers, calculated for long voyages in the California, Australia and East India and China trade. In the district of Bath, some thirty ships are contracted for, to be finished within the current year; while at Richmond, Bowdoinham, Augusta, Hallowell and Gardiner, greater activity than is now exhibited in their respective yards were known before.' Five of his crew of fourteen were also from Maine, including Second Mate Loammi Ross and Stephen Perrington, who was possibly a distant relation of the captain. Accustomed to life at sea but not necessarily to passengers, the men spent a month unloading cargo, fitting the ship out for the use of emigrants and enjoying fresh provisions for the first time in seven weeks.

Meanwhile, most of the Frisians were taking advantage of their time in the city, although the Schaafsma family, who weren't keen on the *William and*

Mary, decided perhaps emigration wasn't for them after all and returned to the Netherlands instead. Roorda recollected that 'At this point our cases and belongings were loaded onto carriages at the station building and transported to a house in the city, which appeared to be primarily a lodging for emigrees and kept by friendly Germans; it was here that we spent the entirety of our stay in Liverpool for two English shillings, which is FL1.20 in Dutch money, per day. Although this spell in Liverpool was not unpleasant for us for the expense it caused us, our accommodation suited us very well and we ate and drank altogether with eighty-five in number at two tables in one shift.' Haagsma also spoke well of the place and said, '[We] soon recovered from the cold we endured on the train.' Bekius, however, was less positive, writing that the boarding house 'proved so unsatisfactory that we had to supply our own food'. He cheered up somewhat later, saying 'we had the opportunity to inspect the city. It was hilly in some places. We saw many splendid buildings some with 3 or 4 stories. But the burning of coal robbed the city of many of its pleasant features. No matter how fine the buildings were, everything had turned black from the smoke of factories; in short, nothing but coal was used as fuel in this city.' This was typical of cities at that time. As Max Schlesinger, a contemporary writer, noted that year, 'English houses are like chimneys turned inside-out; on the outside all is soot and dirt, in the inside everything is clean and bright.'

But the city had great beauty too. Herman Melville, the acclaimed author of *Moby Dick*, spent time there and wrote in his semi-autobiographical novel *Redburn: His First Voyage* (1849), '... in Liverpool there were Chinese walls of masonry, vast piers of stone and a succession of granite-rimmed docks as extensive and solid as the Egyptian pyramids. In magnitude, cost and durability the docks of Liverpool surpassed all others in the world.' Roorda and his fellow Frisians found plenty to do and the glamour and pace of this major city provided something of a culture shock to them.

[We] had plenty of time to see the city and its noteworthy features and went out daily onto the street to this end. The bustle and incredible crowds that I saw in this city were to me a wholly new and strange spectacle; at first we could hardly cross the street for the great mass of all sorts of carts and vehicles, which constantly filled the streets, but gradually I became accustomed to it to an extent; one sees in particular many goods vehicles driving on two wheels, pulled by two extraordinarily large and heavy horses, one before the other, which were steered only by the voices of the coachmen; donkeys and mules were also much used there and these pulled, to our great wonder, very heavy cargos of various kinds consisting of merchant goods; the people seemed to have fruits of seasons all year round, at least we saw all conceivable kinds and new potatoes already on March 4th, in one word everything can be got here; we also saw repeatedly in shops, among other things, all kinds of mounted birds of the most striking and beautiful colours, as well as various mounted foreign species such as tigers and the like.

Haagsma and some of the others visited the races, explaining for people at home, 'They can still be properly called races, while thousands of pounds sterling are spent in betting. The rule is that four horses runs [*sic*] a great distance at the same time and the first to arrive is the winner.' He was less enthusiastic about some of the other experiences he had with English culture, saying, 'We also visited several places of amusement, where we were usually surprized by English inventiveness, but very seldom by beautiful music and song. A harshness pervades English music.'

As in Ely, the traditional dress of the Frisians drew attention. Roorda wrote, 'On our arrival the inhabitants of Liverpool expressed very great bemusement at the clogs that we wore and particularly the oorijzers [a type of head covering] which the women in our company wore, yet nobody was unfriendly to us and the owners of our lodging in particular were always very generous and forthcoming.' Dutch people wore thick woollen socks with wooden clogs and would have clattered across cobbled streets, whereas many of the inhabitants of Liverpool (and the poorer emigrants) would have gone without any kind of footwear due to the extreme poverty there. Nathaniel Hawthorne, author of *The Scarlet Letter*, came to Liverpool a few months later to work as US Consul and was shocked to see people out with bare legs and feet even when there was snow on the ground, turning their skin raw and red.

Haagsma said, 'The Frisian women with their bonnets aroused the pity of the English and they said, "O, God, those women have no hair".' They did, but at that time they cut their hair fairly short, especially compared to British women and wore it under a thin white cloth cap held in place by an ornate metal headdress. These were symbols of wealth and locality and one Frisian woman, 39-year-old Trijntje de Haan, was under strict orders from her mother not to lose hers. Her granddaughter later recalled, 'there was her head dress which consisted of a lace cap with a gold chain over the brow to hold the lace in place and ending at each temple with loops of lace held in place by engraved gold knobs which completed the decoration. Almost the last advice grandmother had received from her mother was this, "No matter how poor you may become, Treen, never give up your head-dress, for without that you will lose caste and your social standing".'

Class and social standing were of great importance to the Victorians, but while some felt reassured by their knowledge of their place in society – generally those in the upper classes – many felt trapped or hobbled by the strictures and snobberies of the system. This was another reason some found the idea of emigration so attractive: the social mobility and chance of a fresh start elsewhere offered opportunities to many that would be denied them if they stayed at home. Thus Liverpool and other ports became inundated with those seeking a better, or at least different, life. Not everyone was happy about this. Nathaniel Hawthorne was displeased with the busy atmosphere of the city, saying 'The people are as numerous as maggots in cheese; you behold them, disgusting and all moving about, as when you raise a plank or log that has long lain on the ground and find many vivacious bugs and insects beneath it.'

Roorda, however, found it stimulating and was also impressed with the architecture if not the atmosphere.

Liverpool has many large and very ornate houses and buildings, many of them furnished with columns of bluestone, as well as extremely large warehouses, six and seven storeys high and supported by stone vaults, also the squares in the city are paved with bluestone. As there are no water courses in the city one can understand how dreadfully dirty and grimy the streets are, partly as a result of the constant driving and walking, especially when it rains this is incredibly awful, while the sunshine cannot penetrate clearly through the smoke and mist of the many steam factories, which in damp weather is so bad that the soot falls to the streets. As the inhabitants receive their necessary water from taps, being the same from the outside as is distributed throughout the city by jacking, the rainwater there is not collected, there are pipes in the middle of every street, through which all the water and waste which falls or comes into it is carried away; these pipes or gutters are always needing repair, so that a few people are constantly occupied with this.

The Frisian emigrants, travelling as they did in a group, seem to have found safety in numbers. Liverpool, in common with other cities, was rife with crime and corruption and people desperate enough to do anything to survive. Those employed within the shipping industry may not have been such blatant criminals but they certainly were not immune, as an 1851 letter to the emigration commissioners revealed: 'The *great* increase of Emigrants introduces a much larger number of brokers and others employed in the trade, who are for the most part chiefly interested in devising modes of evading the intentions of the law.'

The city had built many a fortune upon slavery before it was abolished in Britain in 1834, although only captains' so-called 'privilege slaves' were actually auctioned in Liverpool, in relatively small numbers. Now a different form of human cargo poured through its docks. Figures are hopelessly inaccurate but newspapers in the early 1850s give a general idea of the huge figures involved. According to *The Illustrated London News*, 5 March 1853, 'The number of emigrants who left the Mersey for America and Australia, during the last month, was 12,000.' Despite there being plenty of ships leaving from ports closer to home, as the *Cheltenham Chronicle* of Thursday 3 June 1852 pointed out, 'A very large number of emigrants from Ireland choose the route by Liverpool; the number sailing from that port for the United States is upwards of 20,000 a-month, or a quarter of a million souls per annum. The great mass of these emigrants are Irish and German agricultural labourers.'

The Dutch were often classified as German by the British, just as the Frisians tended to call British emigrants 'Irish', so it is impossible to know which nationality or nationalities the *Liverpool Times* was referring to in June 1852 when they said: 'The transhipment of German emigrants for America still goes on very briskly, as the hundreds of strange-looking people who daily crowd our streets fully testify.... Most of these emigrants are of the very lowest class, but they are comfortably, though coarsely, clad and every one of them can both write and read perfectly.' But, in a time of sweeping generalisations regarding race and breeding and Victorian Britain's attempts to colonise the world, the *Limerick and Clare Examiner* of 5 January 1853 was thrilled to see so many German and Irish emigrants settling in the former British colony.

In addition ... to the original stock, the Celt is the largst [*sic*] element and the German the next – the one imparting fire and energy and the other steadiness and industry within the sphere of their operations ... The American people, consisting as they do, of a mixture of races, but chiefly of the Teutonic and Celtic – the two greatest races of antiquity – are at this moment the foremost, both in physical strength and in intelligence, on the face of the globe. But whatever be the race of the foreigners who visit our shores, the more that come the more rapidly will the greatness and glory of the country be evolved – population and labour being the wealth of nations. No matter what the numbers may be, they will be all absorbed, assimilated, Americanised and become bone of our bone, flesh of our flesh and blood of our blood, just as wholesome food of all kinds and from whatever point of the compass it is brought, when taken into the human body loses its original properties and becomes incorporated with the system giving it sustenance and strength.

While Roorda and the rest of his party enjoyed exploring the Merseyside area and procured provisions for the voyage ahead, other passengers arrived by horse-drawn bus, cart and train to take their place on the *William and Mary*. The ship, chartered by the highly respectable Pilkington & Wilson, was advertised as sailing on Tuesday 15 March, then on Thursday 17 March. For some reason, despite every other ship listed having the captain named beside it, the *William and Mary* didn't. It was also listed as being almost three times larger than it actually was, at 1,500 tons burden instead of 512. This kind of exaggeration and puff was common at the time and accepted as such within the industry, though would-be passengers from rural areas would not be likely to know this was the case. Emigrant guides were often wildly inaccurate and written as if by a person who had never set foot on ship – which may well have been the case. Many people gleaned their information from letters home which were read out in church, diary entries or words of warning or encouragement published in newspapers or posters.

A lot of travellers chose their voyage based on the captain rather than the ship, with some masters gaining fearful reputations for allowing all manner of drunken shenanigans on board or mistreating their passengers – or even murdering some of their crew – while others were renowned for their kindness, professionalism and concern for safety. Good captains also tended to ensure that all provisions taken on board or left over from the previous voyage were checked for contamination, pests, mould and spoiling. Many ships used inappropriate storage vessels for their water supplies, including casks previously filled with turpentine or rotten and green with beards of algal growth. It was not uncommon for passengers to find once at sea that their water was sludgy, alive with worms and with the appearance of pea soup, or that their salt beef was more maggots than meat. Plenty of unscrupulous captains saw an opportunity to profit by purchasing inexpensive 10-year-old casks of pork meant for animal feed or fertiliser, or unused barrels of flour from another ship's hold that should really have been consumed five years prior. Some simply didn't go to the bother and expense of changing barrels if they had any left over from a previous voyage.

There was, in theory, a penalty of 100l. (£100) for bad stores, if they were found on board by an emigration officer while checking and certifying a ship's provisions, but the officers tended to be grossly overworked, especially in Liverpool. In 1851, the emigration commissioners insisted on a report on the state of affairs in Liverpool. They were horrified to learn that ships' water-casks had not been inspected and passengers were not counted on ships not bound for the colonies. Sometimes tickets were collected from passengers who happened to be on board when the officer was present, but more often the number on the proposed passenger list was compared with the maximum number of statutory passengers allowed (i.e., two children under 14 counting as one statutory passenger), meaning that the 'official' emigration figures quoted in countless reports and newspapers were completely meaningless. Sometimes vessels were cleared before the passengers and/or cargo were taken on board, many days in advance of the proposed departure date. Some were cleared while the ship was leaving the dock and people and their luggage were being hauled on board.

Unfortunately for the people boarding the *William and Mary*, the officer who provided Captain Stinson with a certificate of clearance enabling him to leave port without facing a fine or prosecution didn't check the ship thoroughly, including the provisions – and the lifeboats. The officer couldn't have known it at the time, but this decision would prove very costly indeed.

Another issue that would affect the emigrants was the lack of a surgeon on board, although the Dutch party did include a doctor and midwife. Instead, Captain Stinson intended to make do with a booklet he kept in his breast pocket. Even if he had hired a surgeon, that may have been no greater help to the hundreds of people now dependent on him for survival. According to the *Northern Whig* of 1 June 1852, 'the loan of a diploma for the passage is not unusual … our unfortunate countrymen [are] being left in the charge of quacks, when properly authorised Surgeons are supposed to be employed.' Small wonder that in 1847 Charles Dickens wrote, 'The whole system of shipping and conveying these unfortunate persons is one that stands in need of thorough revision. If any class deserve to be protected and assisted by the government, it is that class who are banished from their native land in search of the bare means of subsistence.'

However, the passengers were unaware of the problems in their future and excited about the prospects of their trip, although Haagsma did say, 'Our baggage was not handled as well as we might have wished, but that is the usual manner of the sea-folk.' The passengers were examined before leaving the port, although this only involved a cursory look and perhaps a question of 'Are you well?' from the doctor involved. Haagsma recalled, 'we were towed from the dock up the river by a steamboat. There a doctor came aboard who declared all passengers to be fit to make the trip.' Roorda wrote, 'our departure was delayed from one day to the next, until it eventually took place on March 24th, when the anchor was raised and we left the city. Soon we saw the wide open water once again before us; our departure gave us the new but glorious sight of a large number of ships that arrived at or left the harbour under sail and steam, mostly being towed by steamships.' Bekius was impressed too, saying, 'To my eye the ships to be seen here in the harbor were practically not to be counted. Every 5 minutes one of the steamboats that plied the river steamed away.'

In addition to the 208 passengers now settling into their home for the next six and a half weeks, the *William and Mary* also carried crockery and 'a part cargo of railway iron – a species of freight dangerous in small or inferior vessels and far more so in squally seas along the perilous coasts of the south' (*Athlone Sentinel*, 8 June 1853). This would make the ship more difficult to handle in stormy weather, but for now the day was bright and beautiful and the passengers and crew were happy.

Sailor Stephen Perrington later said, 'We weighed anchor on the 24th of March and set sail on the same day from Liverpool, bound for New Orleans; the wind was favourable and the passengers seemed happy in anticipation of a pleasant and prosperous voyage. The wind continued favourable for us two or three days, until we were safely out of the channel, which is most dreaded by seamen. Nothing transpired after this worthy of note for some days ...'

But when it did, it was fatal.

Chapter Three

[W]e sailed along with a good North-Easter along the chalk-cliffs on the coast of [Wales], which displayed a profusion of lights and shadows. It was the first time we saw the sun disappear behind the waves, which is one of the most beautiful sights once can imagine in nature. The following morning it reappeared beautifully in the waves to the east and we floated along slowly because there was almost no wind. The motion of the ship soon caused people to become seasick ...

(B. B. Haagsma, passenger)

Leaving British and Irish waters, Thursday 24–Wednesday 30 March 1853

There were many tonics, powders and supposed preventatives and patent remedies for seasickness on sale to emigrants and other seafaring travellers in the 1850s. Some contained ginger and other innocuous ingredients and if they did not cure the malady at least they did no harm. Others were as likely to upset their stomachs as the combination of ship-board fare and the motion of the waves. One contemporary emigrant wrote in the *Gloucester Journal* of 9 July 1853,

> Marmalade is a nice relish and can be taken when the stomach refuses other food ... Cayenne pepper is a good stomachic and it is said by some to prevent sea sickness if taken in quantity. I used it freely and suffered but little ... I believe there is no real cure for sea sickness, but by living on plain wholesome food a week or so beforehand and getting the system, if possible, in a healthy state, it will, to a certain extent, if not wholly, be prevented. Avoid rich or greasy food before going and after getting on board.

The passengers on the *William and Mary* suffered terribly and were so afflicted that their quarters were unable to be cleaned of vomit and probably worse until the majority were well enough to leave their berths around a week later.

Haagsma was among the few unaffected but his countryman, 23-year-old sawmill worker Sjoerd Bekius, 'suffered so that for nine or ten days I consumed nothing but cold water. I hardly dared to cast my eyes heavenward.' He was lucky that the *William and Mary* appeared to have relatively fresh water at this stage. In the *Stamford Mercury* of 17 June 1853, one traveller advised others 'to drink as little water as you can, as the water gets very bad and makes many ill. A little brandy is a very good thing to bring. Take a spoonful and mix with a cup of water, it kills the water and takes off the bad taste.'

Bekius got better, '[a]fter having spent 14 days in this fashion in my bunk I finally appeared on deck. My appetite was slight and whatever I wanted to eat I could not retain; but fortunately my former health improved so that my former strength gradually returned' but, although he described all the emigrants as being 'in good health' when they first boarded the ship, some had gone into an upsetting decline.

As Bekius vomited and others groaned in their berths, their fellow travellers settled into their new home. Roorda later wrote,

> The barriers around the ship were five feet high; up on deck at the front was the sailors' quarters, followed by the kitchen for the crew and next to it the passengers' kitchen, this was also the place of the cabin, the two rooms for the steersmen and the captain's bedroom, while the sails and ropes were stored up on deck in a separate place behind the cabin. We were 208 passengers on board, consisting of our company of 87 Frisians and the rest mainly Irish and a few English and Germans, while the cargo in the hold was predominantly rails and unrefined iron.

Their accommodation, in direct contrast to the steamers the Dutch, German and Irish passengers had endured on their way to Liverpool, was below deck. He continued,

> Mr Bonnema had insisted that our company should have an area together and separate from the remaining passengers, as a result of which all

the Frisians and twelve Germans were together in one compartment, separated from that of the savage Irish by a wooden panel, so that we had complete freedom among ourselves.

The garrulous and noisy Irish, English and Scottish passengers were treated with suspicion by the more conservative-minded Frisians. Many of the Dutch group were teetotal whereas the others were happy to indulge in whiskey, beer and porter while on board. As Nathaniel Hawthorne wrote in 1854, '[The British] keep up their animal heat by means of wine and ale, else they could not bear this climate.' If it didn't warm them, at the very least it distracted them from the monotony of the voyage and reminded them of the flavours of home.

One traveller wrote in *Lloyd's Weekly Newspaper* of 13 August 1854, 'So far as regards selecting your society on board … that is done almost imperceptibly. The quietly-disposed soon draw towards each other and separate themselves from the unruly.' The Frisians, in common with Mormon groups who also tended to emigrate on Pilkington & Wilson vessels, had simply separated themselves from the others before setting out.

Roorda continued, 'our bunks were in rows, two rows above each other along the sides of our compartment, in front of the bunks were our cases and chests that served at the same time as benches and tables'. The beds tended to have a wooden plank bordering them, intended to designate berths and keep their occupants in place as the ship rolled across the sea. On their first night at sea, these boards proved wholly inadequate and as Haagsma later recalled,

In the evening we went to bed [and went] to sleep very soon as if we were rocked in a cradle. But, no! At three o'clock at night there was a cry: 'Oh, Lord, we perish! To the life rafts! To the life rafts!' Such was the cry of distress in the dead of night. Almost all of the passengers were awakened and in what kind of situation do you suppose we found ourselves? Eight strong muscular young fellows sleeping on four upper berths rolled among those sleeping below them and paid them an unexpected visit. They raised the cry mentioned above …

At first the wind favoured the ship and the *William and Mary* progressed well, leaving Roorda to say 'the prospect of a speedy journey heartened us all, on the afternoon of the 25th we could still see the Irish coast, but on the 26th all land was out of sight and we saw nothing other than air and water around our ship'. That day there was further excitement on board when the number of passengers swelled from 208 to 209. An unmarried Irish woman gave birth to a healthy daughter, assisted by two members of the Frisian party.

Dr Johannes van der Veer was one of the oldest on board at 56, but his wisdom and experience would prove vital for many on the *William and Mary*. He had previously worked as a barber, saddler, vet, amanuensis (a kind of literary assistant) and instrument maker and seemed able to turn his hand to anything. His wife Sandrina remained in the Netherlands with their children while he sought to settle with Bonnema's party in Iowa. The midwife assisting him would have also been a highly respected member of the community. Childbirth was the second biggest cause of death for women of childbearing age after consumption (TB) and infant mortality was also high with approximately fourteen deaths in every 100 births. Midwifery was a specialised occupation, sometimes pursued by men too and often passed down within families. The Irish woman and her daughter were very lucky to have such excellent support on board.

The otherwise mild-mannered Haagsma was outraged by the woman's behaviour, saying,

> It is really no wonder that in England the people label the Irish as cattle. At least, this woman did not exhibit much in the way of human traits, because when our doctor asked her about her condition the next morning and if she needed anything, he received the answer that she was in need of nothing. She had an abundant supply of something to drink. But what do you suppose she had to drink? Whiskey, my reader, being a very intoxicating drink, which she had been drinking like water.

Roorda even claimed she lay drunk in bed two hours after giving birth. Despite the wooden panel separating the groups, the passengers were still living in very close quarters, although Roorda was grateful for any distance, saying 'it was fortunate for us that we were not in the same compartment … both because of their dissolute and awful lifestyle and because we noticed that everything of ours that came within their reach disappeared instantly and we could not get it back.'

Then the weather worsened, with the wind changing direction, forcing the crew to tack against it, zigzagging onwards through the rolling waves. As Haagsma said, 'Toward evening … the wind became stronger, so that we could soon call it a moderate storm. The next morning the waves increased gradually until they became enormous masses of water, which worried the inexperienced passenger.' As crewman Stephen Perrington later explained, 'we experienced a very heavy gale from the south-west, which lasted nearly two weeks; the ship being loaded very deep with iron and that all being in the lower hold, caused her to roll very badly; indeed sometimes it was impossible to get about the deck with safety.' This made many on board, especially those still struggling with what some described as 'sinking sickness', feel very ill. He continued, 'we had two people suffering from nerve-fevers and a few with bad colds. For the former the sea is not much of a help because of the constant tossing of the ship.'

Three-year-old Gerrit Tuininga was dying. The toddler and his big sister, Antje, were suffering and there was little their parents, Johannes and 'Treen', or their three siblings could do to help. Haagsma recalled, 'we awoke with alarm, when one of those who were ill was snatched away by death from his mourning family. The crying of both of the parents, brothers and sisters was too heart-rending for my pen to describe.'

'Nerve-fever', otherwise known as typhoid fever, is a bacterial infection spread by drinking water or eating food contaminated with infected faeces. Gerrit would probably have experienced intestinal pain, headaches that felt like a tremendous weight was crushing his head or cold water was being poured over his scalp, and constipation. When Gerrit died, his mother placed his clothing in the bag she carried her keepsakes and gold oorijzer headdress in. She would soon have other sad mementoes to place beside it.

Elsewhere in the compartment, a young man was sobbing and there was nothing to alleviate his extreme discomfort. After six days of suffering in his berth, 27-year-old Dirk Hofma died in awful pain on Wednesday 30 March. He lost his father as a toddler and his mother Antje stayed behind in Barradeel with his stepfather while Hofma sought a better life elsewhere. Bekius, who was a few years younger than his fellow Frisian, said, 'no pen can describe how his death grieved me … he left a mother for whom he moaned during the last hours of his life. But this was not the last death …'

It is impossible to know whether they and others would have survived if a surgeon was appointed to the *William and Mary* and supplied with a proper medical chest. Typhoid fever and measles, which was also spreading through the passengers, can prove fatal no matter what medicines are prescribed. As it was, the passengers were fortunate to have Dr van der Veer available, although Captain Stinson also attempted to assist, consulting the booklet he kept in his breast pocket and prescribing them ham if they had a fever.

Stinson at least attempted to give comfort and aid to the sick. Many captains chose not to go near them, as, according to the *Glasgow Herald* of 5 May 1854, a Mr Finch told a committee regarding the subject of emigrant ships,

> There was no medical man on board [the *Fingal*]. The captain attended to the sick as well as he could, on the whole, but he did not consider himself bound to look after the health of the passengers and he refused, to my knowledge, to attend to passengers when they were in bad health. The medicines given in cholera cases were Epsom salts and castor oil and thirty-five drops of laudanum and the face was rubbed with vinegar. I represented to the captain that those were very improper medicines for cholera. He told me to hold my tongue. These medicines were administered by the mate, the captain and the steward, but they were afraid of the disease and did not think it was a duty they were bound to perform and they left to any persons of feeling to do what they thought proper.

Good hygiene measures including washing hands with soap and water are essential for warding off the likes of typhus and dysentery in this kind of environment, but facilities like this were a rarity on ships at that time. As a Mrs Chisholm told the *Hereford Times* of 18 June 1853, 'The wash houses, so boasted of, are a perfect sham – dark narrow cupboards, with a sink hole, impossible to stand in, or see in, without the door being open. They are close to the galley and forecastle, where no woman should go and adjoining the water closets intended for the women, but only fit for men's use.' Mr Finch explained to a committee on emigrant ships a year later that on the *Fingal*, 'There were two temporary water closets, but they were soon down. First, the doors were knocked away and there were no means of concealing the person then. They were for men and women indiscriminately; there were no other water closets. After they were destroyed there was a very bad smell below; indeed, you could not stand below owing to want of cleanliness.'

This was a common experience for seafarers in the mid-nineteenth century. Emigrants were advised to take a chamber pot and/or a slop bucket, but unless the sea was dead calm there were liable to be spills, especially when climbing the ladder with it to reach the upper deck, or when emptying it over the side of the ship. That was, of course, if they had the urge to use them. The *Aberdeen Journal* included the advice of an 'intelligent young man' on 1 June 1853, saying 'Guard against costiveness [constipation]. We had more illness from that cause ... than from anything else. The best remedy found on board was a Seidlitz powder in the morning; but such powders must be done up in tinfoil, or they will not keep.'

This was the age of the crinoline and women and girls wore voluminous skirts and – if they had them – giant bloomer underpants that went past their knees. Poorer women stiffened their multiple petticoats with rings of horsehair or rolled newspaper and stored precious items, such as money and important papers, in their corsets and stays while still aspiring to the impractical wasp-waisted ideal. Outfits were constricting, heavy, not easily changed in such cramped quarters and even less easily cleaned despite this being extremely desirable given the numerous vomit and food stains that would quickly accumulate on the many layers of fabric. Depending on the state of the lodging houses where the emigrants had previously slept and the state of the straw that made up their 'donkey's breakfast' bedding, there would likely be fleas and similar pests annoying them on board.

The *William and Mary* was a new ship and while she would have carried some lice, rats and roaches, there is no mention of any kind of gross infestation as some unfortunate emigrants found in their quarters. Mary Crompton, a newlywed on SS *Great Britain* in 1866, was horrified to relate that, '[A rat] came into my cabin as I was going to bed, I jumped onto the berth and waited until Joe came down, then he and one of the stewards had a grand rat hunt but the gentleman escaped through a hole ... [Another passenger was] wakened by one biting her toenails'. Rats, unpleasant as they could appear to their reluctant human shipmates, sometimes proved useful as an alternative food source when provisions ran low. Many a life was saved by the timely appearance of rat stew.

The passengers on the *William and Mary* were also in some ways lucky that there were no livestock on board. Although this condemned them to suffer salted and preserved meat throughout the journey, it saved them from pig faeces dripping from the sties through to the tables and bunks (and faces of unwary sleepers) below and from hearing the shrieks of the animals as they were slaughtered for meat.

Some extolled the healthy virtues of a sea voyage, including a Mrs Chisholm in 1853,

> I consider that its beneficial influence on the health is unquestionable, that it presents charms to notice well worth the dangers to enjoy and that with a wise selection of stores at no serious expense, all deprivation of the comforts usual at home, to any extent worth mentioning, may be avoided. There are beauties in the sunset at sea, near the time and long after, such as you cannot dream or imagine and the sun-rise is, if anything, more glorious still. The atmosphere is of such extreme purity and the distance you can see upwards, so great that you could fancy one shade more and you would look into heaven itself. The moon–light nights equally clear, show myriads of stars you can never see in your own climate.

But while many on board the *William and Mary* delighted in the natural beauty around them, others were too ill – or hungry – to notice. Even with good storage and careful preparation it was difficult to adjust to the provisions that were standard on transatlantic ships. One unlucky emigrant from another ship told the *Limerick and Clare Examiner* of 28 July 1852,

> Our first meal at sea for eleven days was at least half bone and as hard to cut as a cable. It was not only hard but dreadfully salt, but very bad.

One of the passengers told me he saw the casks carefully covered over directly the inspector came on board at Gravesend. I myself saw some salt beef or horse quite green and stinking. A party of six has been served to day to a pound and a half of bone with one pound of sinew on it. The best of the dinner was potatoes and biscuit. R----- could eat nothing else. This party are now talking to the captain and I have no doubt if this goes on we shall have some desperate work. There are enough mutinous fellows on board who will not quietly submit to this filthy offal for food, after they have paid full price for passage money. It is a piteous sight to see the poor children, who throw this stuff out of their plates; and their wretched mothers unable to give them anything except hard biscuit, which their little teeth are quite unable to masticate.

For the passengers on the *William and Mary* it wasn't the quality of the food that was the problem so much as the lack of it, though it was a rare ship that had no complaints about its fare. There were supposedly strict rules specifying exactly what each emigrant could expect, how much of it they should receive and how often, though in reality they were often short-changed by the men in charge of the ship or the galley.

Vere Foster, writing in the *Wells Journal* of 15 May 1852, laid out what an emigrant should by rights expect to be given while on board an emigrant ship,

The quantities of provisions which each passenger, fourteen years of age is entitled to receive, according to Act of Parliament on the voyage to America, including the time of detention, if any, at the port of embarkation, are:-

Water, at least three quarts daily and the following provisions, after the rate per week of – 2 ½ lbs. of bread or biscuit, not inferior in quality to what is usually called navy biscuit; 1 lb. wheaten flour; 5 lbs. of oatmeal, 2 lbs. of rice; 2 oz. tea; ½ lb. of sugar; ½ lb. of molasses.

Provided always that such issue of provisions shall be made in advance and not less often than twice a week, the first of such issues to be made on the day of embarkation.

Each passenger is entitled to lodging and provisions on board from the day appointed for sailing in his ticket, or else to one shilling for every day of detention; and the same for forty-eight hours after arrival in America.

As regards extra provisions, they must depend very much on taste and circumstances. In my recent voyage in the 'Washington,' from Liverpool to New York, I took the following extra provisions, which I found sufficient and which were the same in quantity and quality as I had been in the habit of supplying previously to passengers whom I had assisted to emigrate to America: – 1 ½ stone wheaten flour; 6 lbs. of bacon; 2 ½ lbs. butter; 4 lb. loaf, hard baked; ¼ lb. tea; 2 lbs. brown sugar; salt; soap; bread soda.

These extra provisions cost 10s. 6d.... I consider the above quantities of extra provisions to be plenty, so far as necessity is concerned, with the exception of a little vinegar in summer; a cheese, more flour, a few herrings, some potatoes and onions and, in case of children, many little extras, such as suet, raisins, &c., would be and were found to be, by many of my fellow-passengers, a palatable and desirable addition, particularly during the first fortnight, until the stomach becomes inured to the motion of the ship.

The handles and spouts of all the tin articles [from the list of articles recommended for use by an emigrant and their messmate: tin water can, large tin hook saucepan, frying-pan, large tin basin for washing and for preparing bread, chamber(pot), tin teapot, tin kettle, two deep tin plates, two pint mugs, two knives/forks/spoons, barrel and padlock to hold provisions, small calico bags, towels and rubbers, straw mattrass (*sic*), blanket, rug, sheets] should be riveted on, as well as soldered. Families would do well to take with them a slop-pail and a broom. The bottoms of trunks should be kept off the damp floor by nailing a couple of strips of wood on to them.

The extra articles of clothing most advisable to take, on account of their superior cheapness and quality in this country, are woollen clothing and boots and shoes. Mechanics should take their tools.

Passengers should be particularly cleanly on board a crowded ship, to prevent ship fever from breaking out.

This was easier said than done.

Americans were angry about the many shiploads of immigrants who entered their ports and brought diseases such as ship fever, a form of typhus spread by infected lice and the *Herald* was quoted in the *Freeman's Journal* of 17 April 1852 as opining, quite accurately, that, 'It is the overcrowding of the passenger ships, the want of proper ventilation and plenty of wholesome food and water, together with a disregard of cleanliness and the absence of competent medical aid, that first originate and then spread the contagion.'

As 'a very respectable Gentleman' told the *Roscommon Journal and Western Impartial Reporter*, 18 May 1850, 'If the Emigrant knew all he had to go through, from the day he leaves his native abode, until he lands at his destination, he would dread the idea of leaving home.' Those aboard the *William and Mary* would soon discover how right he was.

Chapter Four

[W]e thought we couldn't be worse off than we war but now to our sorrow we know the differ for sure supposin' we were dyin' of starvation or if sickness overtuk us, we had a chance of a doctor and if he could do no good for our bodies sure the priest could for our souls and then we'd be buried along wid our own people, in the ould churchyard, with the green sod over us, instead of dying like rotten sheep thrown into a pit and the minit the breath is out of our bodies flung into the sea to be eaten up by them horrid sharks.

(*Robert Whyte's Famine Ship Diary*, 1847)

Crossing the Atlantic, 31 March–23 April

The deaths of Dirk Hofma and Gerrit Tuininga cast a pall over the Frisian party. To lose two of their group so soon was devastating. But the mourning associated with these losses could not be given as much attention as the travellers may have wished. The following morning, as Haagsma later recalled, 'we had to cope with another storm'. The emigrants endured the shifting of the ship and ensuing seasickness, tending to the most unwell as best they could as they waited for the bad weather to pass. In the afternoon, however, it worsened and as Haagsma wrote, it was 'followed by a hurricane too terrible for me to describe adequately with my pen. Under such circumstances the emigrant has many inconveniences, since it is almost impossible to be on deck and much less prepare anything to eat or drink. [O]ne person can make adjustments much more readily than another.' His companion Roorda noted that 'the wind continued to blow strongly from the south-west' for the following three days 'so that we could make very little progress'.

The privations they suffered, being tossed about in their berths and unable to partake of their provisions, made things all the worse for those already sick. Added to this was the lack of understanding of the importance of hygienic measures and the dangers of common household practices which were exacerbated by the difficulties of living at sea. One settler from 1847,

Etta Smith Wilson, recalled in 'Life and Work of the Late Rev. George N. Smith: A Pioneer Missionary', *Michigan Pioneer Collections*, vol. 30 (Lansing, 1906) that 'In the morning the good *vrouws* [*sic* – 'vrouwen'] would empty out their night vessels, wash them and stir their pancake batter in them; [mother] could never witness this performance without being overcome with nausea. There were other habits, also similar in nature, but of which delicacy forbids a description.' Small wonder then that mortality on land and at sea was so common.

Hendrik Spanjer, a 35-year-old from Menaldumadeel, died on Saturday 2 April and Gerrit's big sister Antje, aged nine, died the following day, her clothes joining those of the toddler in their mother's bag of mementoes. Some hours later, Roorda recalled, 'the wind began to turn and become less unfavourable for us and from then on the conditions remained quite favourable for us ... [L]ittle happened that struck me as unusual, although a number of passengers, both among my countrymen as among the Irish, mourned the loss of children of various ages'.

The better weather came too late for Trijntje Graafsma, a fifteen-month-old travelling with her mother, father and eight-year-old sister from Kimswerd. She was the third daughter they had named 'Trijntje' and the third Trijntje Graafsma to die very young. Two days later a baby boy, three-month-old Sikke Sikkema from Barradeel, joined the others in death.

Generally on land the Dutch were keen to dispose of bodies as soon as possible and this shocked some Americans, including one who wrote of an unusual event in his diary in 1847,

> The Dutch, seem to think, the sooner the departed are out of their sight, the better. It is sickening to witness their barbarous customs ... I can never forget my feelings on hearing that some bodies of emigrants which were buried on the beach and had been washed out by the waves were left to be devoured by the wolves.

This timeliness was necessary in Britain and Ireland, too, especially in times of sickness, but there was more made of the mourning customs there.

Often bodies were disposed of at sea within a few hours of the death, before rigor mortis made them difficult to remove from their berth and transfer between decks and before putrefaction set in to the detriment of the remaining travellers' health. The smell of a fresh body would also attract hungry rats from the hold and the sight of them gnawing at a loved one would only cause further distress to the emigrants. However, the terrible storm meant it was dangerous for the passengers to venture on deck, let alone spend time there for a funeral. The bodies were probably placed on the deck until it was safe to dispose of them a few days later.

With any luck, the families and friends of Spanjer and the children would have avoided the awful situation a traveller called Henry Johnson experienced, which he immortalised in a private letter to his wife in 1848,

> Anything I have read or imagined of a storm at sea was nothing to this … One poor family in the next berth to me whose father had been ill all the time of a bowel complaint I thought great pity of. He died the first night of the storm and was laid outside of his berth the ship began to roll and pitch dreadfully after a while the boxes, barrels &c began to roll from one side to the other the men at the helm were thrown from the wheel and the ship became almost unmanageable at this time I was pitched right into the corpse, the poor mother and two daughters were thrown on top of us and there corpse, boxes, barrels, women and children all in one mess were knocked from side to side for about fifteen minutes pleasant that wasn't it. Jane Dear Shortly after the ship got righted and the captain came down we sowed the body up took it on deck and amid the raging of the storm he read the funeral service for the dead and pitched him overboard.

While mourning and body disposal was highly ritualised on land at that time, at sea it very much depended on how a person died, who was left on board to grieve for them and the culture of the ship. One passenger, according to the *Glasgow Herald* of 5 May 1854, while giving evidence about his journey on the cholera-ridden *Fingal* to a committee regarding emigrant ships, said 'I heard the sailors refuse to throw some of the bodies overboard; they were afraid of touching them and I consider they objected because they were not paid. In one case the body was not sewn up in canvas before it was thrown overboard; the captain said, "We are not bound to do it; it is only according to courtesy".'

It was common practice for a body to be washed down by the deceased's family, friends or berth-mates, then sewn tightly into their hammock or bedding, or a scrap of sailcloth. As one man told the *Waterford Chronicle* of 3 September 1831, 'it was customary to run the needle in the last stitch through the nose of the corpse', partly to check they were dead but also to help keep the corpse in place within the shroud bundle. They often remained in the outfit they died in, although sometimes layers were stripped off and given to relatives or sold to raise money for any dependents they may have had. Heavy items such as cannon shot were placed at their feet within the shroud, or sometimes tied on, in order to sink the corpse and spare their fellow passengers the unenviable sight of the body being picked at by scavengers including sharks. Sometimes this went wrong, as 'an orphan girl' reported to the *Dublin Evening Post* of 24 September 1839, when the unfortunate Mr Lewis died of fever.

[A]t that impressive sentence in the form of burial at sea, 'We commit our brother to the deep!' [his body] was gently lowered into its ocean tomb. Never shall I forget the sound of splashing waters, as, for an instant, the ingulfing wave closed over his remains!

'Oh! that sound did knock
Against my very heart.'

The coffin, encased in its shroud–like hammock, rose again almost immediately; the end of the hammock having become unfastened and the weights which had been enclosed, escaping, the wind getting under the canvas acted as a sail and the body was slowly borne down the current away from us … I remained on deck straining my eyes to watch, as it floated on its course, the last narrow home of him who had, indeed, been my friend; till, nearly blinded by my tears and the distance that was gradually placed between the vessel and the object of my gaze, it became like a speck upon the waters and I saw it no more!

There are accounts of emigrant ships ravaged by disease having their dead removed with boat hooks and 'stacked like cordwood' in quarantine stations, ready for disposal, but although the *William and Mary* suffered a comparatively high number of deaths for the route and season, there were enough passengers left alive for humanity to prevail. Emigrants were at more risk of catching contagious diseases such as dysentery, cholera or smallpox at sea than on land. Generally at that time mortality rates on ships were approximately 2 per cent, but in bad years they could be 10 per cent or even 25 per cent and above. It is only surprising given the conditions on board emigrant ships that this figure wasn't higher.

Mr J. Custis, a surgeon from Dublin, worked on six emigrant ships and wrote in the *Mona's Herald*, 1857:

> ... take all the stews [brothels] of Liverpool, concentrate in a given space the acts and deeds done in all for one year and they would scarcely equal in atrocity the amount of crime committed in one emigrant ship during a single voyage ... I have been engaged during the worst years of famine in Ireland; I have witnessed the deaths of hundreds from want; I have seen the inmates of a workhouse carried by hundreds weekly through its gates to be thrown unshrouded and coffinless into a pit filled with quicklime ... and revolting to the feelings as all this was, it was not half so shocking as what I subsequently witnessed on board the very first emigrant ship I ever sailed in. In the former instance every exertion was made to save life, in the latter to destroy it.

Charles Dickens is quoted in *Robert Whyte's 1847 Famine Ship Diary* as saying, 'sickness of adults and deaths of children on the passage are matters of the very commonest occurrence' and they were, but this didn't inure their loved ones to their loss, though many found strength in a strong belief in the afterlife. William Watkins, whose account of emigration was included in the *Hereford Times* of 12 November 1853, was deeply affected.

> [W]e have grim death at work and afterwards the awfully solemn burials. Death at any time is an awful termination to this dream of life; but at sea, it is most to be dreaded. Your mate may be well to-day – to-morrow

death may strike him; and in a few short hours the body is placed upon a plank – the burial service is read, a lift, a roll and then you hear a hollow sounding plunge and the deep seas receive the body of those you may have loved dearly. The waves continue their onward course and your friend is gone for ever. There is something peculiarly horrifying in the sound of a body being thrown into the sea – a sound that it would be most impossible to describe, but one that causes the frame to vibrate and strikes terror to the soul, calculated to make us reflect upon our past and present life, so as to prepare for that awful change, which must inevitably come to all of us.

Sometimes the sheer awfulness of a voyage provided a distraction and enabled them to carry on as they had no choice but to do so or die themselves. But different families coped with their grief in different ways and for some travellers the burial at sea of a shipmate was little more than an interesting spectacle. One emigrant's letter, published in the *Inverness Courier* on 17 February 1853, mentions the death of a child on board.

It was in a canvas bag and laid on a board and one of the sailors held the board while the doctor read – and the first mate gave notice to the sailor and he lifted up one end of the board and shot it into the sea. I got into the rigging to see it go into the water. But very bad order was kept. A funeral at sea has very little effect even on the friends, for the corpse is thrown overboard and no more notice is taken.

One man described the problem with burial at sea to the *Royal Cornwall Gazette* of 9 September 1853, saying 'It can matter little to the dead where their bodies repose; but the idea is a painful one, that over the remains of those buried at sea, no tears of affection can flow, or visits of love be paid, to their last resting place.' A maudlin and sentimental view, but a very Victorian one, with the emphasis on the plight of those left behind.

The lack of a physical focal point for mourning may have been a blessing in disguise for some families, though it might not have seemed so at the time. The emphasis on structured grief and sentimentalised bereavement in Victorian society – and high mortality rates – sometimes led to tragedy, such as the one that befell the Mead family according to the *Worcester Journal* of 8 July 1852:

> [S]ix months ago [she] buried a favourite child, for whose death she was inconsolable. She constantly went to Kensal Green Cemetery, threw herself upon the child's grave and wept for hours. She would then gather the flowers that grew over the grave, bring them home and leave them in water till they decayed, when she would eat them. Day after day she thus indulged her grief; and upon returning home on the 15th ult. after visiting the child's grave as usual, she told her husband, children and friends, that she had only a few days to live. She then had the mourning made for her children, which they were to wear for her; and having directed her husband to have the dead bell tolled for her, refused all medical aid, nourishment and consolation, until Friday week, when she fell a lifeless corpse from her chair to the ground. Mr. Obre, surgeon, performed the autopsy and found that the deceased died of disease of the heart, produced by deep affliction.

What the less-favoured children felt about this is not revealed.

Leaving home most likely for good, suffering a form of bereavement but for a country and culture, not just family and friends, was traumatic in and of itself. Some people lived in the same place as many generations of their family had before them, like the Frisian party, and rarely travelled outside their immediate area, let alone to another county or country. Others, like the Brown family in New Lanark, Scotland, or the Stewarts in the north of England, were already internal migrants who moved from town to town for work, so while a move to America would have been a big change for them there probably wouldn't have been the same deep emotional wrench. But to then experience the privations and stresses of a lengthy journey at sea could and often did change a person, hardening them up for tough times ahead. One settler said in the *Wells Journal* of 21 February 1852, 'There [are] many things to be learnt from a long voyage and some unpleasant things to be endured, but it is a good preparation for a rough life when you land.'

As Stephen de Vere wrote in a letter in 1847,

Before the emigrant has been a week at sea he is an altered man. How can it be otherwise? Hundreds of poor people, men, women and children, of all ages, from the drivelling idiot of ninety to the babe just born, huddled together without light, without air, wallowing in filth and breathing a fetid atmosphere, sick in body, dispirited in heart, the fevered patients lying between the sound, in sleeping places so narrow as almost to deny them the power of indulging, by a change of position, the natural restlessness of the disease; by their agonised ravings disturbing those around and predisposing them, through the effects of the imagination, to imbibe the contagion; living without food or medicine, except as administered by the hand of casual charity, dying without the voice of spiritual consolation and buried in the deep without the rites of the church.

Religion was generally very important to people in Europe in the 1850s, though it was also a divisive subject. The Irish on board the *William and Mary* were mainly from the North and likely Protestant, as were the Frisians. The strong religious convictions of the passengers seem to have helped them through their loss. Haagsma noted with approval that, 'On April 10 my attention was drawn to the quiet movements of the crew. No work was done on the ship and the sailor sat quietly reading his testament. From this you can conclude that the Sabbath is observed in quiet reverence by English [speaking] crews.'

Generally speaking, an emigrant ship contained society in miniature – and a highly pressured one at that. The *Gloucester Journal* of 9 July 1853 included a letter from an emigrant detailing what ship passengers might expect on their journey.

Our work on board ship consisted of washing, pudding making, scraping under and in front of our berths, washing up plates and dishes and all other things that usually fall to the lot of the servant of all work on shore. These things can scarcely be called compulsory, only you are obliged to do them in your turn, or pay one of your neighbours to do them for you and plenty can always be got for a consideration, but few like to be thought above doing for themselves. Could our friends have seen us with our shirt sleeves tucked up, scrubbing and cleaning and the style in which we took our meals, they would have had sufficient food for laughter to serve them for some length of time. Plenty of tailoring was done on board – it was a favourite amusement: also shoe cobbling, tinmen, braziers, carpenters, in fact all sorts of trades on a small scale, the butcher and baker included.

Another child was born to the Irish, lifting the spirits as did the steadily improving weather, although Roorda was again unimpressed that the new mother had been drinking alcohol. Giving birth can be a difficult, dangerous and agonising experience under the best of conditions. Safely delivering a child in a cramped and filthy berth with the room tilting around you might seem near impossible, but many managed it nonetheless. Five days before, Queen Victoria had been in labour with Prince Leopold and had rebelled against the accepted idea that a good Christian woman would suffer during the birth of her children. According to the *Coventry Herald* of 3 June 1853, 'A handkerchief, on which a small quantity of chloroform had been dropped, was held to the face. Her Majesty was never completely insensible, but she expressed herself perfectly satisfied with the anodyne effects produced.' This was a world away from the *William and Mary* though and the Irishwoman's alcohol was the next best thing to an anaesthetic as they sailed past the Azores.

Amongst the celebration that day, the death of Baukje Kooistra, a girl of two, devastated her family. One of her brothers was also failing and there was little Dr van der Veer could do. Haagsma later wrote,

I noticed that the captain does a great deal in the way of caring for the sick. The man had little or no knowledge of natural science nor chemistry; but his practical ability was dependent upon a small book, which among other things contains the statement that in case of a fever it is sometimes advisable to eat bacon. Before he would visit his patients he would study in this his trustworthy guide.

Sjoerd Bekius said, 'I thought repeatedly of our miserable condition, for constantly bodies were carried out for burial (in the sea).' These included

British and Irish children, but there was no record kept of whom. One of them was one-year-old Margaret Diamond of Durham, in the north of England. She had been emigrating with her parents, aunts and grandparents for a new life in sunny St. Louis, a world away from the damp colliery towns and villages her family had grown up in. Her parents, John and Susannah, had married while awaiting her arrival and she had been Susannah's parents' first grandchild. This was a devastating blow for their little group, though perhaps not unexpected to the seasoned travellers on board. A contemporary emigrant's diary included in the *Berkshire Chronicle*, 3 September 1853, stated that infants sometimes pined to death 'for want of [their] natural aliment (which generally fails when nursing mothers get to sea)' – unsurprising since the water available to these women was often scarce. In general everyone was growing short-tempered and Haagsma somewhat scathingly wrote,

On April 12 the captain said we had covered 900 English miles in 5 days. Notwithstanding we heard a great deal of argumentation about the duration of the passage. One of our people, not exactly the inventor of the steam-engine, says: We will arrive in New Orleans on Sunday night ... This is according to a labourer.

Thankfully later that day some visitors to the ship provided the bereaved with an entertaining distraction. Roorda said, 'we heard that harbour porpoises could be seen from the fore of the ship, we all ran at once to the front, as on such a long journey every opportunity was seized to reduce the boredom and monotony; these animals looked very much like our own ordinary pigs.'

Those that could do so rushed to the high sides of the ship to watch them dart through the waves, marvelling at their speed and agility and counting fourteen creatures swimming so close they could almost reach out and touch them. Some sailors considered the appearance of a porpoise to indicate a coming storm, but the weather was unremarkable. A different kind of storm was brewing, however and the next day it burst.

*   *   *

The passengers were terribly hungry. Most had paid for half-board, meaning they were entitled to receive a certain amount of rations in addition to food and drink they brought on board themselves. This would, or should, have worked out well enough for them, but from the outset there had been discontented mutterings among the emigrants and suspicions of theft. After almost a month at sea, this became too much for some passengers to bear.

Haagsma noted that,

> Once a week provisions were distributed and in such a way that a half of the ordered portion stuck to the fingers of those doing the distributing which was all loot for the captain and mates. This time one of our people was not satisfied and he accused the first mate of being a thief which prompted the latter to start a fight.

The first mate was Samuel Billings Welch, a 49-year-old from Charleston, South Carolina and probably the oldest crewman on the *William and Mary*. A father of two, he seemed a rough character, inclined to violence and cruelty on board ship. Another Frisian man joined the argument and according to the ever-diplomatic Haagsma 'he received a greeting which was not welcome'. Tempers grew frayed, with other crewmen either coming to Welch's aid or eager to watch the fight and passengers trying to see and the Frisian 'placed his hand on his knife'. Some women screamed, 'He will get killed, he will get killed!' but thankfully 'at that moment the captain interfered and the parties were more or less satisfied'. This did not in any way endear the passengers to the crew. Meanwhile, others snuck away and sought some form of recompense for their lost provisions. As Haagsma put it, 'several young men took advantage of the sugar barrel which had been left unguarded by the sailors in order to help the mate'.

Poor supplies of provisions were common at that time, no matter what checks were performed in port before the ship left. Once at sea the captain was all-powerful and if he did not make a point of ensuring rations of a decent quality were provided to those on board as the regulations specified, there was little the passengers or even the crew could do. A few years earlier 'a very respectable Gentleman' named Edmond Kirwan told the *Roscommon Journal and Western Impartial Reporter*, 18 May 1850, 'The Passengers never can get justice on board an Emigrant Ship until the Government appoint a man whose duty it will be to weigh out the provisions and give out the water and receive complaints'. This was still the case.

While the Frisians were fighting with the first mate, elsewhere another emigrant, a Mrs. Chisholm, was writing about her struggles to eat on another ship. She told the *Hereford Times* of 18 June 1853,

A portion of the provisions are of the very worst description and none above mediocrity. The salt beef too bad to be eaten; fish the same, unfit for human food, the surgeon say; pork, very inferior; the commonest Bengal rice; tea of the coarsest and most tasteless description; great part of the flour mouldy; the preserved fruit is only a quarter of a pound of cranberries, a little more than a wine–glass–full requiring nearly all your sugar to sweeten them. Coffee unroasted, with only one small roaster and that such a poor one that it was out of order in a fortnight; and a trumpery old mill that grinds about a pound an hour.

She also wrote of her encounter with another ship which had an even more unfortunate situation on board,

One day we spoke a ship which came so close as to lock the spars of the two vessels together. Ours broke away with a fearful crash, we thought it was all over with us; the other vessel at length passed ahead without any accident to life or limbs. The crew of this vessel were nearly starving, their biscuits had all gone bad, so that for several days they had subsisted upon treacle. I am sure the Captain was mad if ever man was. His face was covered with hair, so much so that we could not see his mouth till he spoke. He had put the mate in irons and flogged his crew every day. At night he slept with a loaded revolver under his head for fear of being murdered. They were bound to Peru and had been driving about for three months by contrary winds. The Captain's name was Ward; you will perhaps see something of him, either that he is gone mad or been murdered, in the newspapers.

Captain Stinson was, in comparison to the terrifying Captain Ward, a model of good behaviour, but it is easier to present as a decent and competent captain in the middle of the ocean with stores aboard and wind in the sails than it is anywhere else on earth except, perhaps, port.

This situation would not last for long, however, and the *William and Mary* was soon plagued with yet more deaths. On Monday 18 April, 18-year-old Lyckle Tjalsma of Kimswerd died. He was the eldest of six children travelling with their mother, Sjoukje and father, Sjoerd, a professional skipper seeking a new life with Oepke Bonnema's group in Iowa. Lyckle was joined that day in the Atlantic by 16-month-old Marinus Kooistra, Baukje's little brother.

Although the weather was improving, the situation on board the ship was growing worse. On Saturday 23 April, while at least two weeks away from their destination, the provisions began to run out. With no meat available other than rats, the emigrants had nothing but hard biscuit, dry rice and broken peas boiled in water to sustain them. There should have been ample food and water for all. Their situation was growing desperate.

Chapter Five

[A]lthough we are out of the vicinity of sharks, the 'lions of the deep,' yet we have the lively porpoises in shoals, darting swiftly through the sea and jumping up like frisking lambs around the ship and at night dashing the spray in all directions, with their rich phosphorescent colours, giving them the appearance of a mass of rich glowing silvery fire. But all eyes are now strained to catch a glimpse of the 'monster of the deep.' There is seen at some distance a couple of streams of water, sent spouting forth into the air! Again! and it is certainly coming in the direction of the ship. Presently a huge mass of glossy substance is seen to roll its great length along, passing the sides of the ship; ... [the passengers] have seen a whale, in full life and vigour and in its natural element.

(William Watkins, emigrant, *Hereford Times*, 12 November 1853)

The Final Days of the Voyage, 24 April–2 May

For once, fate appeared to smile on the *William and Mary* and the prayers of many were answered as fish literally threw themselves on deck. The flying fish evolved unusual fins allowing it to propel itself from the water, away from predators and glide as much as 20 feet above the surface. Their 'flights' generally span approximately 160 feet but if they catch the updraft at the leading edge of a wave they can cross up to 1,300 feet before re-entering the ocean, travelling at speeds of more than 43 miles an hour. The emigrants were delighted to find some twisting and turning on deck, breaking the monotony of the voyage and a diet now largely restricted to dry rice and hard peas.

Roorda and his fellow travellers crowded the sides of the vessel, enjoying the pleasant weather and watching the sea. He said, 'one mass of very large fish played constantly around the ship, while the water was so clear that we were always able to observe them and see how they dived underneath and then resurfaced'. Once the emigrants had found their sea-legs, the voyage became more tolerable and occasionally even enjoyable. According to Haagsma, 'we entertained ourselves with music or in other ways'. Those with an instrument would gladly show off their prowess with a melody, some passengers – or occasionally, sailors – would sing and dance and there would be a celebratory mood for a while at least as people let loose with a jig.

There were restrictions regarding who could go where on the ship, none more so than for the Frisian women, who were forbidden from going on deck with bare feet. But Captain Stinson appears to have taken a shine to at least one of the young women, as Haagsma later related: 'One evening, at the request of the captain, a Friesian girl was dressed in national or rather provincial clothing and presented to him, which he, the mates and others enjoyed very much. They were especially impressed by the gold ear-pie[ce] with the lace bonnet. The captain called her "a soldier with a southwester." The gold ear-piece he said was the helmet and the southwester, that you can easily guess.'

This visit to the captain and crew appeared to go well, though there were later intimations of unwelcome advances from the sailors to the girls and women on board and even some mutterings of sexual assault. If this did indeed happen, as is likely, then the victims would not have been encouraged to complain or even acknowledge what was done to them. They would have been subject to gossip and probably considered at least partially to blame and there would have been little chance of justice on board – or on land.

*   *   *

As the *William and Mary* continued to sail south-west toward New Orleans, the weather grew steadily hotter, the sea more predictable and the travellers sweatier. There was only so much washing possible with a rag and a bucket of salt water. Roorda recalled, 'it was frequently calm again and so warm there that a number of our passengers entertained themselves by swimming in the sea'. What some thought was a tan built up by weeks lived on the open ocean, with the sunlight reflecting off the water and intensifying the damage done to their skin, soon came off after a good soak and revealed their true complexion.

This would have been a new experience for the emigrants; even those who had lived in coastal towns such as Ebenezer Miller of Dundee were unlikely to have done more than paddle, at least in public. This would often have been done while wearing 'normal' clothing, with women lifting their skirts and many layers of petticoats a little and men rolling up their trouser-legs or donning special bathing suits. Beach visitors would have paid to use 'bathing machines', little wooden huts fitted with shafts and mounted on high wheels, towed into the sea by horses. Segregated by their gender, they would have climbed down a small set of steps into the water, perhaps shielded by a canopy from the view of other beach-goers and the harsh effects of the sun and helped into the water by an assistant. It was a completely different experience to the fun they would have near the ship.

Sailors would usually take the opportunity for a swim to also wash their clothes, swishing the garments through the water, taking care not to let them go and watching the ingrained dirt and crusts of salt sluice away. They would pass the clean clothes back onto the deck, throwing them up into a sodden heap if they felt confident of a successful aim, where their flannel shirts and wide-legged trousers would be draped around the coils of rope and hung off the sides to dry. If there were females on board, they would either be confined to their quarters or sailcloth would be used to shield the naked bathers from view.

This cloth was also employed to assist those less used to ocean bathing. As Richard Bentley, who described himself as an 'Emigrant Churchman', wrote in 1849,

> The best swimmer has been known to be appalled at the thought of the measureless depths beneath and to go down like a stone. A sail, however, is sometimes sunk five feet or so below water, extended from between the fore and main yard-arms, which affords a wonderful protection even from sharks and other monsters of the deep, though these are not so much to be dreaded in the latitudes traversed by vessels on the North American passage as on that by the Cape.

There had only been the usual galley and human waste thrown overboard for a week, no bodies in makeshift shrouds plunging into the depths of the Atlantic and revealing the ship to be a source of nourishment for sharks and other large predators, so those who decided to go for a swim were relatively safe.

The periods of calm that allowed the travellers to swim in the water unfortunately meant the ship was lying still, with barely a breeze in her sails. With few provisions left and little chance of more fish flinging themselves on deck, some of the more astute passengers began to grow uneasy. It was difficult for the most experienced captains to accurately work out where they were on the open ocean without a single speck of land in sight, let alone a fairly new captain such as Stinson and several passengers were convinced he was keeping them at sea for too long.

Some crewmen began to sneak drinks of alcohol, becoming unruly and unpleasant. With the passengers growing ever more hungry, thirsty, bored and restless, it was only a matter of time before the ship erupted with violence. Then, on Friday 29 April, another girl died. Three-year-old Maaike Sikkema was the twelfth emigrant to die on the *William and Mary* in the five weeks since the ship sailed from Liverpool. Fifteen days prior, her little brother Sikke had joined the others in the depths of the Atlantic. Their sister Grietje had died as a baby the year before in the Netherlands. Their parents were now childless and grieving, hemmed into their berth by families and suffering terribly. Another unnamed emigrant, an adult, had died in the British and Irish section of the ship and this exacerbated the situation. Mourning traditions on land had little merit when those stricken with grief were at sea. A poem by 'M.J.S.' included in the *Roscommon Journal* of 11 July 1835 encapsulates some of the attitudes and rituals common in the early to mid-1800s.

> … they wrapp'd his corpse in the tarry-sheet,
> To the dead as Araby's spices sweet,
> And prepared him to seek the depths below,
> Where waves ne'er beat, nor tempests blow.
> No steeds with their nodding plumes come here,
> No sabled hearses, no coffined bier,
> To bear with parade and pomp away
> The dead to sleep with its kindred clay.
> But the little group, a silent few –

His companions mixed with the hardy crew,
Stood thoughtful around, till a prayer was said
O'er the corpse of the deaf, unconscious dead,
Then they bore his remains to the vessel's side,
And committed them to the dark blue tide:
One sullen plunge and the scene was o'er,
The wave roll'd on as it roll'd before!
In that classical sea, whose azure vies
With the green of its shore and the blue of its skies;
In some pearly cave, in some coral cell,
Oh! the dead shall sleep as sweetly as well
As if shrined in the pomp of Parisian tombs,
When the east & the south breathe their rich perfumes.
Nor forgotten shall be the humblest one,
Though he sleep in the watery waste alone;
When the trump of the angel sounds with dread,
And the sea, like the earth, shall yield his dead.

Tensions were running high and hunger wasn't helping. Then, as Roorda put it, 'At the end of April we experienced – alas! – a fearsome exercise in punishment on board.'

When passengers were allotted their provisions, they then had to somehow transform their tin mugs and bowlfuls of dry peas, rice and ship's biscuit into something they could actually eat. This meant spending a considerable amount of time acquiring water for cooking (often seawater hauled over the side of the ship), boiling it over a fire, mixing ingredients together, then dividing the resulting fare amongst the family or group it belonged to. With over 200 people on board requiring meals several times a day and only a cramped and overheated galley at his disposal, the ship's cook, Peter McDonald, had a very difficult job. Everyone wanted their food and hot drinks served quickly, for their portions to be larger, for the meals to taste better or at the very least for the rations they received to be edible.

But stores were running low and there was still no sign of land on the horizon. There was a very real risk of them dying of starvation and the only answer was for the mate to reduce the amount of provisions given, despite the unhappiness of the passengers and crew. After the recent fight between First Mate Welch and some Frisian passengers, regarding the theft of their food and drink, the passengers knew there would be little chance of assistance from the crew. The ship's cook, neither sailor nor passenger, was a different matter.

McDonald was under tremendous pressure and eventually he seems to have caved in. He was accused of giving some of the captain's sweet pudding to the British and Irish passengers. This, if true, was an understandable but terrible mistake on his behalf. It was dangerous to go up against the captain of any ship and Stinson was not a man to be crossed.

A ship was an unforgiving location, often peopled with brutes, where the captain was god, judge, jury and sometimes, executioner and his crew could either follow orders or face punishment themselves. As R. H. Dana quoted his captain as saying in his 1840 account, *Two Years Before The Mast*, '"Now, my men, we have begun a long voyage. If we get along well together, we shall have a comfortable time; if we don't, we shall have hell afloat."' Dana was a sailor and pointed out the dilemma that faced many at sea when disagreeing with the captain, 'If a thought of resistance crossed the minds of any of the men, what was to be done? What is there for sailors to do? If they resist, it is mutiny; and if they succeed and take the vessel, it is piracy.' Both mutiny and piracy were punishable by death.

In a ship full of pent-up frustration and anger, McDonald's alleged redistribution of food was the perfect excuse for the crew to let rip. He was dismissed from his post, another man being appointed in his place and threatened with prosecution upon reaching port. But then there was the problem of what to do with him.

Information is limited regarding what happened next. There are rumours of prolonged torture, McDonald having an iron bar thrust into his mouth while he was tied up and savagely beaten on deck. Bekius and other Frisian men apparently witnessed the aftermath, protesting to First Mate Welch when they found McDonald lying in a pool of blood, arguing that he should be tortured no more and threatening to tell the captain of this heinous act – only to be told that the beating was the captain's orders and if they complained they could expect a dose of it themselves!

Roorda described it as 'a severe beating' and with precious few medical resources available on board, McDonald sounds lucky to have survived. Having received his initial punishment, he now had to wait to see what befell him on shore, but there was no knowing how long that would be yet.

The mistreatment of McDonald was a shock to the passengers, despite their earlier experience of the crew's volatility, especially since it was done at the captain's behest. It would have been no surprise to anyone who knew mariners though, including the author Nathaniel Hawthorne, who wrote in 1855,

> There is a most dreadful state of things aboard our ships. Hell itself can be no worse than some of them and I do pray that some New-Englander with the rage of reform in him may turn his thoughts this way. The first step towards better things—the best practicable step for the present—is to legalize flogging on shipboard; thereby doing away with the miscellaneous assaults and batteries, kickings, fisticuffings, ropes'-endings, marline-spikings, which the inferior officers continually perpetrate, as the only mode of keeping up anything like discipline. As in many other instances, philanthropy has overshot itself by the prohibition of flogging, causing the captain to avoid the responsibility of solemn punishment and leave his mates to make devils of themselves, by habitual and hardly avoidable ill treatment of the seamen.

This was progress from the days of Queen Elizabeth, when, according to a chaplain quoted in the *Leeds Times* of 7 April 1838,

> mutinous sailors were tied up in a bag and hung at the bowsprit end, with a biscuit, a bottle of beer and a knife; so that when the culprit was tired of his situation, he might release himself from it by suicide, either cutting his throat or cutting the bag and falling into the sea … [Another punishment involved] suspending him from the yard arms by the heels, (while the ship was rolling) at sea; so that, in the course of half an hour, the repeated thumps against the ship's side would not leave a whole bone in his skin.

Keelhauling was only made illegal the year Roorda and his friends sailed on the *William and Mary*. Since it was primarily used in the Dutch Navy, although Bonnema's company would perhaps have been aware of it, McDonald avoided this awful fate. A grisly punishment for minor infractions at sea, it involved the hapless mariner being dragged below the keel of the ship using a rope passed under the vessel. As ships were encrusted with barnacles and other rough marine growths, rubbing against the ship – especially at speed, or with force – would result in deep cuts and possibly the loss of limbs, genitals and facial features and even decapitation. Sometimes the unfortunate crewman would be weighted with chains or pulled slowly enough that their body would sink to a sufficient depth to allow them to avoid the surface of the vessel, but this would often lead to them drowning instead. The blood loss from open wounds would also attract predators such as sharks.

The purpose of McDonald's punishment was twofold: to admonish him for his supposed theft of the captain's food; and to serve as a warning to those on board who might be tempted to misbehave. It worked.

* * *

The passengers noticed that their captain was now growing more impatient, pacing around the ship as if nervous. He had good reason to be. They should have sighted land by now and with supplies of food and water growing ever more reduced despite the loss of 5 per cent of their passengers, there was a pressing need for them to reach their destination and avoid hazards such as sandbars, shoals, rocks and other shipwrecks that peppered the shallows near the coast.

There was a strong wind blowing, filling the sails and sending the *William and Mary* speeding through the waves. Unfortunately this would lead to disaster. As Haagsma later explained to his friends,

[T]he wind was from the north so we could not reach the proper channel without difficulty. The only approach possible would be to turn back and then sail in. But, alas, the captain did not wish to turn into the New Bahama canal ... [T]he crew had continued to go south, so that it was not possible to sail along the north side of the island, into the New Bahama canal, but where the gulf was available to us.

Exactly a week before the *William and Mary* left Liverpool, another American-owned emigrant ship had made the same mistake. The *Osborne* of Kennebec, Maine, was also sailing from Liverpool for New Orleans when the ship became a total wreck on the island of Grand Bahama. The captain refused to leave the vessel until all his crew and the 240 passengers on board were rescued and managed to save part of the cargo, too. Experienced mariners who had sailed around the Florida coast knew to avoid sailing through the group of islands known as the Bahamas and the shallow channels there had their depths and larger rocks clearly marked on maps and charts, but Stinson decided to attempt the route regardless.

Most of the passengers were unaware of the peril he was putting them in. Roorda later said,

When we approached the American coast around this time we were excited as if in rapture at the appearance of the sunset; never had we seen anything so magnificent in the heavens in our homeland and it is impossible to describe the sight of so innumerably many colours in the clouds, with which it was accompanied, never had my eyes observed such a magnificent natural phenomenon.

Although land was not yet in sight, the clouds that gather over land masses were apparent in the sky and a source of comfort and relief to the passengers and crew. 'In the morning, the 1st of May, we received the happy announcement by our captain that we would reach the islands on the following day and that after we had reached them we would complete our journey within 4 or 5 days', recalled Bekius, but '[i]n this also we were disappointed.'

The passengers crowded the sides of the ship, craning their necks, keen to be the first to sight land. Londoner Joseph Brooks, who was emigrating with his wife, told how 'all went well until the 2d of May, when our troubles began to commence. On that day the captain told me he expected to make the land before dark; but not doing so orders were given to keep a strict look out forward.' It was just as well that he did.

Chapter Six

[T]he stars, when I sat down, were shining brightly overhead and everything indicating a fine evening. A sudden gust aroused me from my reverie and starting up, I saw for the first time, a heavy cloud approaching. In another minute, the sea all around the ship was lashed into foam, each wave lighted up with a myriad of phosphorescent coruscations, but I dared not stay long to admire the beauty of the scene, for the sails overhead roared as if they were going to ribands; ropes and stays were loosened and flew about in all directions, which the darkness rendered unsafe. I hurried below and had scarcely crossed the threshold, when down poured the rain in torrents and some of the more tardy ones who followed me, were drenched to the skin and minus their caps. In half-an-hour afterwards the sea was as calm as a mirror and except the streaming decks and dripping sails, there was nothing to indicate its late violence. Such is a tropical squall.

(Contemporary emigrant account,
Berkshire Chronicle, 3 September 1853)

Approaching the Islands, 2 May–3 May

The ship sailed ever closer to destruction, while hundreds slept in sweaty bunks below. A captain and his crew could relax somewhat when out at sea with not an obstacle in sight and land many miles away, but with charts indicating that the rocky outcrops of the Bahamas were near, Stinson couldn't help but grow anxious. The wind that filled their sails swept the *William and Mary* into the shallow channel through the islands and the crew were alert to the sounds of water breaking against something other than the sides of the ship.

According to Joseph Brooks, '[t]hree of the most intelligent men were placed [at the front of the ship to keep a look out] and the captain told me he should not go to bed before daylight'. The ship's lookouts stared into the darkness, seeking any indication of land, such as the lights of a settlement or beacon, the pale froth of waves rushing and retreating on a beach, or the solid black of a low island against the navy sky. As Haagsma recalled, at midnight 'they expected to sight land at any moment. We were sailing straight west with a strong north wind and had only 3 or 4 ship lengths to go before striking the Bahama shore and face certain death.'

Then, as Brooks later said, '[a]bout 12 ½ o'clock at night, the captain told the mate he was certain that land was near, as he could tell by the peculiar sound of the water. The mate ran forward to look out and, sure enough, the land was near. He instantly came running back, ordering the helm to be put hard to port and to call the watch to brace round the yards; telling the captain that the land was not more than one mile ahead – we going at the time at the rate of seven miles per hour. A man was instantly sent aloft to see if he could make out the Hole in the Wall-light; but it was not caught sight of …'

Haagsma wrote, 'as soon as land was in sight, the captain rushed to the helm and in a moment turned the prow to the southwest and we were saved'. Already a teetotaller, Haagsma was grateful for the captain's sobriety, especially with so many lives at stake. 'I thought about the responsibility a seaman has at a time like that and for the first time realised how important it is to abstain from the use of a strong drink. I was glad the captain did not have liquor on the ship for the crew, because, how many shipwrecks are caused by human indulgence in that beast-like lust, is a secret which some day will be revealed.' Unfortunately, Haagsma and the others would soon find that a sober crew was not necessarily a moral or brave crew – though the addition of liquor would undoubtedly make a difficult situation worse.

The Bahamas are a group of low-lying islands, with few natural landmarks for sailors to guide their ships by and plentiful hazards needing to be avoided. There were a couple of lighthouses in the area but bad weather sometimes put them out of action and there were rumours of islanders sabotaging them too. Ten years before, the *Cheltenham Chronicle* of 25 May 1843 published an account of a voyage to New Orleans, which the *William and Mary* was attempting to repeat.

We were roused rather early by the cry of land and dressed in as great haste as the heat would allow, to be on deck in time to see the lighthouse on the island of Abaco, which we passed at about five miles distance and the Hole in the Wall, a cavern 30 feet high, which passes entirely through a rock running into the sea. It is an object eagerly watched for, being the first point of land seen on this voyage. Abaco is a rocky and barren island belonging to Great Britain, containing no other inhabitant than the tenant of the lighthouse.

A wrecker was sailing about and would doubtless have been glad to make our gallant bark a prize; but a fair wind wafted us safely on. The morning was bright and warm and the colour of the sea a lovely aqua marine and when the sun shone through the tops of the waves, showing a richer green, edged with white foam, this together with their graceful motion, struck me as most beautiful. I could have gazed on each succeeding wave for hours without satiety.

We passed the Berry Islands about noon and saw very distinctly the palm-thatched dwelling of the black governor 'Old Jack', and his many wives, who are also his servants, sailors, &c., for besides himself there is no man on these islands. They are 10 in number, low and green, with clumps of dwarf cedars and looked pretty as the foam dashed peacefully against the rocks and the sea gleamed in white lines on the coral reefs between them.

We were now on the great Bahama bank, another wonder of the deep, which if the seas were to pass away would probably appear an immense mountain covered with peaks and ridges and ravines, suddenly terminating in a precipice many miles deep, now filled by the gulf and stream. The soundings are in many places very shallow and the ridges are easily seen by the pale green (almost white) colour of the water. When deeper it is blue and these alternate streaks have a singular effect. The navigation being dangerous here, our captain wisely dropped anchor at eight o'clock, in 18 feet of water and remained till four in the morning; though the breeze was fresh and fair and we were sorry to lose it, yet we felt this delay was preferable to being driven in the dark on the Orange Keys, some dangerous rocks near us. During the night, a brig came up and anchored alongside of us.

Tuesday had but little interest or variety, excepting what I could find in gazing on the pale green sea, so clear that I could distinctly see fishes gliding along and large masses of sponge at the bottom. There were also numbers of flying fish looking very like small white birds. A shark 10 feet long was then caught and once partly hauled up the stern, but the hook was bad and it escaped.

The warm waters and abundant marine life in the Bahamas meant the area was filled with many species of sharks, including great hammerhead, tiger, nurse, black tip, lemon, silky and bull sharks. Well fed on fish, they would still investigate with their mouths anything that appeared in the water near them, especially if it made a sound or bled, so the passengers of the *William and Mary* stayed on board despite the heat.

Soon they saw islands to their right and happily predicted that their voyage would draw to a close in but a few days' time. As Bekius later said, 'On the morning of the 3d we saw lights which gave us indescribable pleasure because as much as ten days ago we had eaten our last meat and since had subsisted on dry rice and hard biscuit. We also had broken peas boiled in water with nothing whatsoever added; but as we had nearly reached our destination such privations were quite bearable. In the morning, about 7 o'clock, we passed the islands which presented a pleasing sight. We no longer entertained any thought of danger.' The pitiful rations seemed that bit more bearable now the end was in sight.

The passengers chatted to each other and the crew about their plans, what they hoped to achieve in America and where they sought to go. Margaret Walsh, a 25-year-old from Ireland, was meeting her husband, a farm labourer in Washington. The Stewart family from the mining districts in the north of England were aiming for the pits of St Louis, while 50-year-old Prussian Catherine Burns and her 15-year-old son Henry were returning to his home state of Philadelphia. The Sullivan family were leaving poverty-stricken Ireland to labour in Niagara. Illinois-bound Phillip and Hugh Fitzpatrick were two of six siblings from Meath, Ireland, to settle in the US leaving only their eldest brother behind. Patrick and Rosa Ryan were heading for Galena, Illinois, to stay with family. Ebenezer Miller, 26, had left his somewhat unusual family of adopted children in Dundee, on the unforgiving east coast of Scotland, to seek his fortune in the States. Tjipke Algra, 25, was travelling with his wife Pietje, 28, as part of Oepke Bonnema's party to Iowa to work as a farmhand and scores more were going with them in search of a different, and hopefully better, life.

One of the older men in the Frisian party, 56-year-old Siebren Wesselius, later recalled, 'When we saw a western island, being very happy because we were told that we would reach New Orleans within four days. Our happiness was however of short duration.'

Some, like Haagsma, had reservations about the course set. '[W]e found ourselves in the Providence canal. It was certainly hazardous for the captain to enter a canal 20 ft. deep with a vessel drawing 17 ft. of water. Only one hidden rock at 3 feet would be enough to determine our eternal destiny.' Generally the channel was more than deep enough for a relatively small ship like the *William and Mary*, at between 1,000 and 1,500 feet, but there was the very great danger of running into the sudden shallows of the Great Bahama Bank, where the Northwest Providence Channel meets the Straits of Florida. Haagsma was right to be concerned.

The correct and sensible procedure upon entering such a shallow and treacherous area of water would be to proceed slowly, with the utmost caution, while constantly sounding the depths and comparing the measurement recorded using a weighted line and also the sediments embedded in the soft wax contained in the weight to the mariner's chart of the area. As soon as the lead was brought up from over one side of the ship, the line measured and the wax examined and cleaned or replaced, it should more or less immediately have been dropped from the opposite side. As the captain plotted their progress with the map, the crew would be alert to any shoals or outcrops through the clear water and assisting with the steering of the ship. This didn't happen with the *William and Mary*. On the contrary, Roorda noted, 'the ship made fast progress and consequently we had the firm hope of being able to sail through the Bahama canal that evening'. The weather grew steadily worse, clouds obscuring the sun, racing across the sky with the wind and the sea became dark and choppy.

Another child died, adding to the anxiety on board. Four-year-old Rinske Westerhuis, named for her deceased grandmother and elder sister, was travelling with her three brothers and their parents from Het Bildt as part of the Frisian group. As R. H. Dana noted in *Two Years Before The Mast*, 'Death is at all times solemn, but never so much as at sea. Then, too, at sea, you *miss* a man so much. There are no new faces or new scenes to fill up the gap.' But instead of dwelling on the loss, the crew and many of the Westerhuis's fellow passengers had to maintain their focus on the perilous situation they found themselves in, in order to avoid joining little Rinske in her watery grave.

*   *   *

The Bahamas were an increasingly attractive area for British and Americans, as the *Berkshire Chronicle* noted on 4 June 1853,

> The Americans are beginning to find out that the Bahamas have a health-restoring climate; and the governor of these islands, adverting to the fact of the arrival of invalids from the United States, says, that English health-seekers might find it worth while to try a season in the same sunshiny latitudes. Another light-house has just been built on one of the islands, whereby navigation among the reef-bordered channels is greatly facilitated. If our fashionable M.D.s will only take to recommending the Bahamas, the governor will soon find himself surrounded by troops of the valetudinarians.

But the few lighthouses positioned amid the treacherous shoals and cays were of no use to those on board the *William and Mary*.

Captain Stinson was also growing ever more worried about their position. He later recalled, 'At sunset about 7 o'clock, the weather became very thick and the wind increased in squalls.' Joseph Brooks, a world away from the London smog he grew up with, remembered that, 'Towards dark, the captain gave orders to shorten sail – wind blowing fresh from southeast. About 8 o'clock, the captain came on deck and told me he should not go to bed that night, as he was in a very dangerous place. He showed me the position of the ship by tracing in a rough manner her course with a penknife on the deck. He said that near about was a sunken rock and he did not know exactly where he was. From this time, he began to be visibly agitated. I spoke to him, but could get no answer.'

Other passengers noticed the captain's demeanour, among them Bekius, who noted that, 'hardly were the sun's rays hidden from us when the sails were furled and put disposed of. Only a few were left unfurled and to us the captain seemed uneasy. This soon appeared justified.'

Roorda, along with many of his party, was looking forward to a swift conclusion to this leg of their journey, but not everyone was so optimistic. He later wrote how, 'in the evening, I was sitting talking with one of my companions about our journey, which we had successfully completed up till now and we could now cherish the expectation that we had covered effectively the entire distance. Some passengers were buoyant, others were filled, as it were, with a dark and anxious premonition, heavy and entirely downcast.' This foreboding proved entirely justified.

Bekius later wrote that,

[W]e suddenly heard what sounded like a thunderclap. This was followed by a severe shock and we were stranded on a rock. The wind rose so that frequently the ship began to roll. Our only thought was that in a few moments we would find our grave in the waves. The number of the unfortunate people on board was more than 200 among whom there were 12 sailors. We sent up a few rockets that a nearby ship might see us, but alas! Every hope for help proved futile. Imagine, my friends, this dreadful situation – how the children clung to their parents and how parents clutched their children – in short; we stood by helplessly and overwhelmed with sorrow.

Another Frisian, 27-year-old Hendrik Jans Kas, was terrified and said, 'soon there was some leakage and we could already see the water [entering the ship]. Everyone was terribly frightened about such a collision against a rock and we were all in fear of death. We saw nothing in store for us than death. For if there was no escape we would all have our grave in the waves and no one saw a chance of being rescued.'

The passengers experienced the initial jolt of the wreck in different ways depending on where they were in the ship. Brooks, who was on deck at the time, said, 'At 8 ½ o'clock, the ship struck. She did so very gently and so still did she remain that I thought she was off again.' whereas Roorda, sitting with his companions in another area of the deck, recalled that, 'we suddenly and unexpectedly heard a huge rattling sound, the ship lurched and sailed over a wave that was at least six feet high at the crest: immediately it lay still and shortly afterwards a second wave came, the back end of which lifted the ship up and brought it down square on the submerged rocks. A deadly fear gripped us, we now ran down below and then back up among the core of passengers who thronged on deck.'

Wherever they were in the vessel, above decks or below, there was now a dangerous atmosphere of panic and terror. With around a dozen sailors hastily assessing the damage, grabbing tools and supplies or clambering into the rigging and adjusting the few sails still open to the ferocious gusts of wind, all while avoiding the 200 passengers on deck and attempting to listen for shouted orders over the screams, the *William and Mary* and all aboard her appeared doomed.

As is often the case when someone experiences a traumatic event, crewman Perrington remembered the events surrounding the wreck in great detail. After conversing with a number of the passengers, who were in high spirits and looking forward to seeing their families and friends in America very soon, he

> bade them good night and in obedience to the command of the mate went aloft and helped furl the mainsail. After executing a few other orders, it being my lookout, I went forward and relieved it, as near as I can remember, about half-past 8. When I stepped on the forecastle I heard the mate order the lead to be carried forward. The man just picked it up and got forward with it when she struck. Orders were given immediately to brace the yards round, which was done as soon as possible without effect. By this time the passengers were all on deck, running and screeching, 'We are lost! We are lost!' and crowding the deck so that it was almost impossible to get from one part of the ship to the other.

As Haagsma put it, 'sure enough, we discovered that our captain had miscalculated, when the keel scraped along the hard sand ... with a loud crackling sound … We noticed that the bottom was clearly damaged. Everyone expected to perish at once. The cries and scramble were terrible.'

Stinson later stated that, 'judging ourselves to the northward and westward of Great Isaacs, [we] kept the ship west by south and commenced heaving the lead … At 8.30 sunk on a sunken rock and hung about midships, with ten fathoms water all around. After pounding heavily about fifteen minutes she went off and struck on another rock within a few rods [about 10 metres] of the first …'

The *William and Mary* was now impaled on a rock in a sea swarming with sharks, 1,200 miles from home.

Chapter Seven

We had all retired to rest, when, a few minutes after twelve, crash went our ship on a coral reef! shaking us all nearly out of our bunks and the terrible reality bursting upon us that we were wrecked in the middle of the ocean. 'We're wrecked! we're wrecked!' exclaimed many, rushing up on deck in their shirts. I sprung out of bed and quickly got on my trousers, coat and shoes and rushed on deck. Here what a scene did we behold! All around us as far as we could see by the starlight, was one sheet of foam. To windward were the gigantic breakers coming on with race-horse speed, every minute or so striking the ship with terrific force, lifting her up and letting her fall again on the coral rock, crunching it beneath her and the water rushing over the side, nearly washing us away as we clung to the ropes and belaying pins. Some few were cursing the captain, others groaning and crying, many praying, friends clinging to one another determined to perish in each other's company ... every crunch went through us like an electric shock. Wet and frightened, we spent the hours until daylight in misery and wretchedness, not knowing how soon the vessel might break and launch us into eternity; many spent the precious time in prayer and in reading comforting passages in the Bible; such hours of misery I would not willingly pass again for all the gold in California.

(Robert Silcock of Chesterfield, *Derbyshire Courier*, 19 March 1853)

Disaster at Sea, 8.45 pm 3 May–7 am 4 May

The crew rushed to their stations as fast as the crowd of panicked passengers would allow. Some of the more able emigrants, who had experience of sailing themselves or had spent time studying the crew as they worked and talking with them throughout the voyage, joined them. One passenger, Joseph Brooks, later wrote, 'As soon as she struck, the helm was put hard up and order given to brace round the yards [the wooden spars sails hang from]. The mate eased off the larboard brace [rope] and the men loosened the braces on the starboard side; but that was all they did and the braces and yards were left swinging to and fro all night. Soon after she struck, the captain inquired of the mate whether she went ahead at all. "Not a d—n bit," was his emphatic answer. The next order that was given, was to clear away the boats, which I assisted in doing.'

By adjusting the angle of the sails, the crew were changing how the gusts of wind hit the vast expanses of canvas billowing above their heads. The sails could drive the ship more solidly onto the rocks, blow the masts over – ripping the ship apart – or help them manoeuvre off the cay and into open water again. Leaving the ropes to dangle as the massive wooden spars swung to and fro added unnecessary hazards to an already dangerous environment.

With no natural light to guide them, only lanterns showing them the way, the men hastened to let down the boats currently dangling from davits. There were five boats on the *William and Mary*, nowhere near enough to hold the 200 men, women and children on board or the provisions they required to stay alive until rescued. This was typical for the time, but that was little comfort to the people involved.

The storm was still raging around the ship, waves crashing against the high wooden sides and splashing the people thronging the deck. The boats, which had lain all but unused as they crossed the Atlantic, had to be cleared of stowed gear, tools and other items before the men lowered them into the water. With a bit of luck, these could be used by some of the travellers to seek help from the nearby islands or a passing ship, or at least assess the extent of the damage and judge whether they could repair it. Crewman Perrington said, 'The two life-boats were launched first and four men got into the starboard boat, taking with them two cans of water, a compass and some bread. They remained in the boat all night and with the greatest difficulty kept her from being stove [in]. The larboard boat was safely launched and but about half an hour after was stove under the quarter. This was caused by the decks being so crowded aft that the boat could not be dropped astern.'

If the boat had been lowered at the stern of the ship, it would not have been at such great risk of smashing against the long sides of the vessel. Unfortunately, the boat lowered on the left or larboard side was too close for the waves to safely toss about and became holed under the waterline. If there had been sailors in it they may have been able to guide the boat away from the hull and out of immediate danger, but with only a dozen sailors on board the *William and Mary* and several already in the other lifeboat checking the damage and with three other boats needing launched and the main ship requiring considerable work, this was not an option.

Another one didn't even make it to the waves before it was in trouble. The so-called 'jolly boat' was generally used for transporting goods and people to and from the ship, or for other small excursions. This one was hanging near the rear of the ship. Passengers climbed over each other to get into it, weighing it down and ignoring the crew's pleas for them to get out so it could be safely lowered into the sea.

One young Frisian, Izaak Roorda, described what happened next:

On one side of the ship a boat hung from iron supports or brackets as thick as a man's arm; this boat was at once so greatly filled with passengers that these thick irons drooped right down to the water, at which the waves struck against the boat with such force that they had to climb out again, in which we assisted them with much energy and effort. It was fortunate that this boat did not end up so fully laden in the water, as it would then surely have sunk immediately, for the passengers, mostly women and children, were sitting literally on top of each other.

When they had all left this boat I immediately got in it with three more of my fellows, barely knowing for mortal fear what we would do; the waves of the sea frequently rolled over it, which obviously left us soaking wet; several times the captain, steersmen or sailors took it in turns to come and hit us with sticks and poles, attempting thereby to drive us out, but we refused to be moved by this; until at around 11 o'clock a wave broke off that end of the boat where I was sitting from the dinghy berth.

Fortunately I had a rope in my hands just then, which I grabbed and held on to as the boat fell away beneath me; my situation at that moment was terrible, one moment completely engulfed by the waves, the next completely above them, all the while hanging so far out of the ship that nobody could help or save me, I would certainly have found my grave here, had I not, by slowly letting the rope slip, finally been able to reach the dinghy with my toes and fortunately it drifted or swept a little closer towards me on a wave, so that I could reach it and let go of the rope.

The three who climbed into the boat with me and who were sitting at the other end of it, had meanwhile been able to climb from the dinghy onto the ship, I had ended up at one end of the boat, but because they were stuck at the other end, they lost their balance and managed to stand upright, from which I was again completely submerged under the water, while at the same time I held on tightly to the side of the boat, so trying to clamber upwards, which I managed to do and finally, after the greatest effort, came back on the ship and so was saved from an immediate and very great danger to my life.

A fourth boat was lowered and this was successfully placed into the roiling water, but the passengers' hopes of escaping in this small vessel were dashed because, as Joseph Brooks later said, 'We had orders to let her go astern, which we did; but when they came to where the [jolly] boat had swung into the water, the two boats dashed one against the other and both were stove in.'

While all this was going on, elsewhere on the ship some crewmen were bustling to and fro between the stores, the galley and the cabin, stowing provisions and supplies of water away and refusing the passengers access. Some of this was passed down to the sailors in the lifeboat along with a compass, before the boat was allowed to drift away, tethered to the *William and Mary* by a rope.

Given that there was no way of knowing if there were more rocks nearby that the *William and Mary* might receive further damage from, it was reasonable to remain anchored in the dark and to prepare a smaller vessel for the morning. If Stinson was unsure of where they were on his chart of the channel or what hazards were around them, the sensible course would be to use one of the smaller boats to find a passage through, at least until they were able to reach a place of comparative safety and repair the ship or ferry the passengers ashore. But this wasn't the reason for Stinson and the crew's preparation of the little boat, as the emigrants would soon find out.

Some of the passengers attempted to use the pumps to return some of the water rushing below decks to the sea, but the crew initially refused their help. Families clustered together on the deck, screaming for salvation, plucking at the clothes of the crew as they rushed past. All was confusion.

Captain Stinson's worst fears had been realised, but all was not lost – yet. He squeezed between the crowds of howling emigrants and grabbed papers from his desk, seemingly at random, which later apparently proved to be a pile of worthless bills. He could have taken the logbook, the list of passengers, charts … anything but useless receipts. But this is what he later claimed to have done. Eventually he attempted to organise – or perhaps distract – the passengers, as well as the crew. Brooks later recalled that at midnight,

[a]bout three hours after we struck, the captain called all the male passengers together and told them that he expected that as the tide rose the ship would float off the rock and that if they would try and keep the vessel afloat until the morning, by working at the pumps, he would then be enabled to run the ship on shore, where everything would be saved. Accordingly, we went to the pumps and worked as men whose lives depended on their exertions.

While the more able-bodied passengers were labouring at the pumps on deck, the crew were busy elsewhere. As Stephen Perrington explained afterwards,

The long boat was still remaining on the after-house, unfit to be launched without caulking. Part of the crew were ordered, however, to get that ready and the remainder to lay forward and get ready to cut away the mast. The ship was now rolling very heavily, the sea breaking over her every few minutes during the squalls. Some of the headstays were cut and every thing got ready to let the foremast go overboard, but the Captain gave orders not to cut it, as the sails kept the ship from rolling. We were then ordered to lay aft and do what they could to get the longboat ready to launch, after which we commenced caulking, tearing up our quilts to get the cotton to caulk [stuff gaps between the planks] with. We had been here but a few minutes when she went off the rock; all expected she would sink immediately. Her anchors were let go as soon as possible and after drifting a few rods she struck again so heavily that it prostrated many on the deck and it was evident to all that the ship could not possibly stand but few more such shocks.

The scene was now dreadful beyond description. Some were upon their knees praying for the Lord to have mercy on them – some were crying, others were running, catching hold of the officers and crew, begging them to save them, telling them that they were unfit to die – that they were unprepared to meet their God. Some who had the evening previous been boasting of their infidelity were the first upon their knees and loudest in their cries for God to have mercy on them. It now seemed evident to all that the ship would go down immediately. Men who before this had acted their part nobly now ceased to make any effort to save themselves or others. – Some went to a cask of liquor that was between decks and there forgot their dangers and troubles.

The mate and myself went below about twelve to ascertain, if we could, the amount of water in the ship. It was then but little above the keelson [a beam fastened lengthwise above the line of the keel to add strength to the structure of the vessel], much less than was expected. We informed them on deck immediately, which seemed to encourage the hope that the ship might be kept afloat until some assistance could be procured. They labored more earnestly at the pumps and those who were willing to work were kept caulking the long-boat. It was almost impossible, in fact, to get them to work, as they despaired of saving themselves.

Emigrant Joseph Brooks stated that, 'the mate came and told us we were all right, for he had been down in the hold; there was only three feet water there and that we were reducing even that. We now felt somewhat at our ease and anxiously waited for daylight.' Roorda, already sodden from his lucky escape, also recollected his time on deck all too well.

Barely had I returned to the great ship than I and many passengers took to the pumps: fear, anxiety and shock drove each of us instinctively to look for a means to save ourselves; the scene on board our ship at that time was heartrending, wailing and groaning filled the air, many of us fell on their knees and called loudly on God for mercy and pity, others climbed into the masts; it is impossible to form an image of our terrible and hopeless situation, the cabin filled with people and when an enormous creaking sound was heard in the ship below, we thought the whole vessel would sink immediately into the depths. Notwithstanding that we were stuck on the rock and since there was still some hope of being saved that in my view could only be achieved through trying to lighten the ship and so float again and so at around 12 o'clock the anchors were lowered; all this time the ship lurched incessantly and heavily, so that we feared it would overturn; there was no equipment to send out distress shots on board, the emergency lantern was beyond use, neither were emergency arrows to send signals into the darkness to be found, so we found ourselves at dead of night without any hope of help or rescue.

The crew worked constantly on the boats to restore them and prepare them so that they would be seaworthy when they took to the water, throughout this time we had to pump water constantly, the water we pumped out was as brown as beer from the ship's cargo, one can imagine what extremely tiring work this pumping was, because of the dreadful swaying and bumping of the ship, the waves rolled over the side where we stood and the water flowed up to our knees, yet despair gave us strength.

Some of the passengers continued to toil at the pumps as others prayed aloud in several languages and people on the nearby islands slept on, unaware. A few hours later Perrington and Samuel Welch made an unwelcome discovery, 'The mate and myself again went to the hold to find out whether the water was gaining and found that there was some seven or eight feet of water. We still endeavoured to encourage the passengers to work at the pumps, hoping that she might be kept afloat till daylight.'

Captain Stinson appeared to be losing his nerve. A more experienced or able master might have kept a better command of the dozen crew left on the *William and Mary*, or taken advantage of the able men among the 196 passengers he was meant to keep safe. Instead, the passengers were having to keep the ship afloat, their companions calm and the captain from leaving them. Haagsma watched Stinson as he strode around the ship, still wearing his slippers and with a spyglass in hand and noted that, 'The damage to the bottom was not so serious that we could not keep the vessel afloat with pumps for quite some time. [But t]he captain seemed to think otherwise, at least he tried all night to get into the life-boat which was drifting in the sea a short distance from us. He was continually prevented by the crowding of the people. The pumping was zealously continued throughout the night which saved our lives …'

The hours passed in sweat, tears, swearing, praying and desperation. Communication was hampered by the noise and the crowds of people separating some of the crew. First Mate Samuel Welch was unaware that all of the boats in the water, save for the lifeboat, were holed. As his fellow crew member, a panicking Stephen Perrington, recalled, the mate 'got into it and attempted to bail it, but making no progress, he was finally compelled to give it up. He then got into the life boat, not daring to return on board the sinking ship, which was at this time rapidly going down. I got into one of the boats that was stove and hauled myself along by a rope running from the ship to the life-boat, into which I got. I was followed by John Best, who jumped overboard and swam to the boat, which was now about as full as it would hold. The spray was breaking over it.'

John Best told the *Spirit of Democracy* of 1 June 1853 that he 'was standing on the side of the vessel just as the rope which held the boat was about to be cut and asked the mate if he should jump; but receiving no encouragement from him, he was about giving himself up for lost, when he thought that by rendering some service he might be allowed to get into the boat. Knowing that they were in want of a sail, he took one of the ship's skysails and handed it to those in the boat, who, although the boat was already overcrowded, could not refuse him a chance for his life.'

This abandonment did not go unnoticed. Brooks said, 'At 5 o'clock I had occasion to go aft and was surprised to find that the first and second mates were in the boat that contained the four sailors. This excited my suspicions and I went to Capt. STINSON and accused him of intending to desert the ship, but he said he intended no such thing and that if we would keep the pumps going he would not leave the ship.'

Indeed, Izaak Roorda later wrote that,

Slowly daylight broke, which gave us some consolation that quickly developed into a faint hope when the captain made Mr Bonnema the firm promise that he would not leave the ship before all the people were off and would then leave together with Mr Bonnema and Dr Van [*sic*] der Veer.

When the day was fully risen we could detect land in the distance; although it was too far away to be able to reach it in the boats, we still cherished the hope that someone there would perceive our miserable situation and come to our aid, yet the emergency flag that had been raised hung, alas, behind a sail in such a way that anyone on land could not see it, the sails were not tied, by which the swaying of the ship was caused to a great extent and at the same time we were in danger all the time of a rope, a block of a piece of wood being hit, even the masts were not cut away, which would otherwise have considerably reduced the swaying.

A little time later that morning we saw the lifeboat, which had been lowered from the ship, on the sea, with the two steersmen and six sailors in it and this led us to the terrible suspicion that they had abandoned the ship, leaving us to our awful fate; yet the captain told us that there was plenty of hope, as the ship was afloat again and they would do what they could, he asked us to keep up the pumping, as many of us were doing.

Captain Stinson may have made a firm promise to the senior members of the Frisian group, but he was altogether more threatening to others, telling Haagsma, 'if you pump you will live, if you do not pump, I will leave you to your fate.' This was an odd thing for Stinson to say. There was a general expectation that a captain would be among the last to abandon a ship in trouble, not least because of the importance of honour and a certain code of chivalry at sea to people of the time. There were also complex legal issues involved with willingly surrendering command of a vessel to others who might then claim ownership or salvage rights and incur expenses for the owners. The passengers grew increasingly suspicious that they were about to be left for the sharks and waves to take care of. 'Even the captain was without hope, but he nevertheless promised us not to abandon the ship until the last passenger had left it,' noted Sjoerd Bekius, 'But alas! in this we were deceived.'

The treacherous captain now directed the passengers' attention to the launching of the longboat and, as an appalled Roorda said,

> At this the captain signalled to the steersmen and sailors who were in the lifeboat, who immediately approached, at which he got into it. A sailor who also tried to get into the boat was threatened with death should he dare to do so; the captain then told those members of the crew who stayed behind on the ship to try to save themselves as best they could with the big boat and having waved with their hats they left, causing the despair of several passengers to rise to a peak.

The captain, who had taken the time to change his slippers for sturdier sea-boots before deserting the men, women and children in his care, stood for a few moments with his hat raised in parting and Hendrik Jans Kas even overheard him call over to them, 'Friends, may you fare well.'

Stephen Perrington, a distant relative of Stinson, watched him clamber into the tiny vessel and later attempted to excuse the master's actions.

> The captain was the last who got into the life-boat and even then he had to be urged very strongly before he would consent to leave the vessel. When the passengers saw him leave the ship, they knew there was no longer any hope and became perfectly frantic with despair, screaming and calling wildly for that assistance which it was impossible to render them.

Stinson later stated, after much clamouring from concerned relatives and the press for answers, that through the night the weather was 'black and squally' and that at 7 am there was 10 feet of water in the hold.

> [T]he ship [was] going down … the passengers abandoned the pumps in despair and finding it utterly impossible to save the whole of them it was with great difficulty that I could induce them to launch the longboat, so great was their fear of being swamped. I should state at this time (7 a.m., 4th of May), the Great Isaacs bore east-south-east six or seven miles, the wind blowing heavy from the south-east in squalls,

so that it was impossible for us to have reached them against the wind and sea unless we ran the risk of losing the lives of those we had been so fortunate in saving from the sinking vessel. The only resort now left us was to keep our boats before the wind and the sea, in the hope of reaching the Florida coast. Half an hour after we left the ship she disappeared and we supposed that she had gone down, together with, probably, 170 passengers and one or two of the crew and the ship's steward.

He lied.

Perrington gave more detail and hope, when he spoke, but also hinted at the horror of what happened next to those left on board the *William and Mary*.

As soon as the captain left, six of the crew, who still remained in the ship, got ready the long-boat, into which several of the passengers jumped indiscriminately. I never saw anything in my life so fearful. Women and men jumped overboard from the after part of the vessel near where the boat lay and many were drowned. One of the crew who was in the long-boat was compelled, with a hatchet, to keep off the passengers who were crowding into the boat and who, if allowed to enter it, would undoubtedly have sunk it. We cut our boat loose from the vessel, rigged a sort of sail and ran before the wind.

Back on the ship, the remaining sailors hastened to lower the longboat, having spent the night poking cotton from ripped quilts between the planks making up the boat. Roorda watched them prepare the craft, 'after first having brought in three buckets, a few containers (all these for baling [*sic*] out) and one blanket'. Then,

[W]hen I saw that they were letting the boat down, I hastened to the rear of the ship above the cabin, just as the boat went down into the water, hardly had I got there than I leapt immediately into it, over the heads of those who were in front of the barrier; a large number of our unfortunate colleagues were walking along the barrier on deck, but had no time to climb over it and thereby throw themselves into the boat.

In an instant twenty-seven of us in number found ourselves in the dinghy, among these were just three of our company of Frisians, being Ulbe Bergma [sic] from Pingjum, Onne Martinus Wagenaar [sic] from Heerenveen and myself, the rest were almost all Irish [i.e., not Frisian or German]. Out of genuine fear that at the least movement of the ship, the boat being so full of people that it would necessarily sink, the sailors quickly cut the ropes and in 2 or 3 minutes we were free from the ship; while we set down one of our unfortunates leapt into the sea, beat his hands on the side of the dinghy, at which we pulled him back in.

All of a sudden a wave dragged us so far from the ship that it was impossible for anyone else to jump into our boat; yet even though another four people, two men and two women, leapt into the sea, surely out of wild despair, for us it was an awful sight to see these stricken individuals wrestling with death with no way of saving them that would not bring us all in danger of our lives; whenever we tried to approach the ship in order to reach them, we found ourselves in great danger of our boat being thrown against the ship by the force of the waves and dashed to pieces, or of so many shipwreck victims leaping into it that it sank; so we had to leave these four unfortunates to their fate in the hope that they would be saved by the remaining passengers on the ship, which we could not yet observe, the women lay still on their clothes, the men splashed and dabbled about in the sea. It is impossible for me to sketch the mental state I was in when we rowed away from the ship, on hearing the heartrending wails which went up from those people who remained on board, around 170 in total, even though we could not understand what they called out as we ourselves were in a state of agitation and numbness, nevertheless we heard that their cries of need and fear were far greater than before and, of course, because for them now all hope of being saved by the boats had disappeared.

Sjoerd Bekius, still on the deck of the stricken *William and Mary*, was horrified. 'I saw [four people] drown. I stood speechless and nearly fell down unconscious and prayed God that then and there He might cut off the thread of my life so that I might not witness the catastrophe which was at hand.' His fellow countryman, 56-year-old Siebren Wesselius, was horrified too, later writing to his son-in-law in Michigan that 'they left us. Dear children, I cannot begin to write you the cry of anguish and horror which then ascended.'

The usually calm and coherent Haagsma was apoplectic with rage at the sheer awfulness of what he witnessed, later writing that Captain Stinson

conducted himself in a very selfish manner ... [disappearing] at the very moment when the large boat was being lowered into the water; at the very moment when many were eager to leap into it – at the very moment that a man drowned – at the very moment that another young man who missed the boat but still attempted to climb into it, lost his fingers when a rude crew-member made use of an axe and drowned as a result – at the very moment that a woman was thrown from the boat into the water, who was bewailing the fate of those who were drowning, with sympathetic tears and similarly became the victim of those monsters – at the very moment when a man parted from his wife and children forever – at the very moment ... but why recall more of the horrors? Only because I wish to write in detail, I must do so.

Accounts vary depending on factors including how distraught a person was or where they were located and the view they had. It seems clear, though, that at least three unnamed men and women died attempting to gain access to the longboat or, in the case of one young woman, from being deliberately tossed overboard for being vocal in her upset at watching others struggle and drown in shark-infested waters and witnessing a crewman (possibly Isaac Ridley, a 21-year-old from Harpswell, Maine) chop at the hands of her fellow passengers. The longboat was dangerously low in the water, carrying far too many people, with the sea seeping in through the cotton-wadded gaps in the planks and sometimes sloshing over the sides, too. There were twenty-eight men, women and children depending on luck and the skills of the four sailors among them – they perhaps felt they couldn't risk her capsizing the boat and dumping them all in the water and hoped that she would somehow, despite the fashions of the time meaning she was probably wearing a tightly-fitted corset and approximately sixteen layers of clothing, swim back to the main ship. Whether the men whose limbs were hacked at with the hatchet lost their fingers, hands or arms, they were murdered just as surely as she was.

Haagsma also pointed out another reason for the ship staying at anchor for so long despite land being in sight and standard procedure for the time being, as Stinson himself had said, to allow a wrecked ship to beach on the nearest shore. 'Before the captain left, he had dropped the anchor, in order that we might not be witnesses of his evil deed, having become victims of the waves.'

Haagsma, and others, believed that Stinson had deliberately left them on the wreck to die.

Chapter Eight

When the barque William and Mary *sailed from Liverpool on the 24th of March last, the emotions of her passengers were alternately shaded with sorrow and hope. All must have felt the national grief which unnerves the stoutest heart on leeving* [sic] *for ever the homes of their kindred and committing themselves to a distant land and an unknown destiny, while hopes must have in return exercised its soothing dominion and reassured the timid as well as the brave that Providence had in store for them a brighter lot and at any rate their fortune could not be worse under an American than an Irish sun. – The poor emigrants could not then anticipate the lamentable disaster which floated so many of their corpses on the coral reefs of the Bahamas – a fate which might well afford a warning to such as would commit themselves to the perils of a distant voyage, anxious to escape from one set of evils only to experience another and more painful class; and should they reach the goal of their wishes, perhaps to lament the fatal intrepidity that tempted them from home in search of an improved condition, pictured by fancy, but fading away before such realities as the going down of the* William and Mary … *Captain Stinson provided for his own safety and that of his crew. He obeyed the primary law of self-preservation, but he appears to have been in too great a hurry to yield to the instinct. Having missed his reckoning and brought disaster on the emigrants by his ignorance of the channel he was bound to make some other efforts for the safety of the passengers. Our emigrating countrymen are constantly deceived and duped and in their hurry to fly, take little care either of comfort or safety, provided any kind of transit is secured … It were well if many more looked far and thought deeply before venturing on such fatal voyages …*

(*Athlone Sentinel*, 8 June 1853)

Panic Ensues, 4 and 5 May

At first the two boats managed to stay together despite the pitch and toss of the sea and the panic of those on board. A total of thirty-six people had succeeded in escaping the wreck of the *William and*

Mary, including almost all of the crew, but the tides and currents of the Atlantic as it swirls around the approximately 700 islands and cays that make up the Bahamas soon separated the vessels.

The waters around the Bahamas and the relatively nearby coast of Florida formed part of a busy shipping route, so there was every reason to hope that in time they would be spotted by some of the clippers, steamers and fishing vessels that travelled there every day. The *Freeman's Journal* of 31 May 1853 went so far as to describe the area as 'a general highway to vessels bound south'. But just because the emigrants had survived the initial chaos of the *William and Mary*'s collision with submerged rocks and the chaos of launching the longboat, it didn't mean they were safe yet.

Having stayed up all night, terrified and engaged in the hard physical labour of pumping, they now had to contend with the dangers of an overfilled boat letting in a lot of water in a sea filled with sharks that investigated anything interesting with their mouths. Some of the emigrants, who had thought their families and friends were right behind them as they scrambled into the longboat, were wracked with the awful guilt that comes with leaving loved ones to die.

But, as Roorda said,

> We had no time, however, to contemplate these sad scenes for long, as we immediately had to plug the leaks in our boat and [bail] it out to prevent ourselves from sinking, while we also had to take all possible care to stop it capsizing, since it had lain on deck in the sun for the duration of the whole journey and was so dried out and the seams torn so wide open that we could see through them, though here and there it had been repaired at night, nobody could possibly have caulked everything given the great disorder and short time we had.

Five women were on board the longboat: Catherine McGuire, Bridget Higgins, Bridget Boyle, Rosa Ryan and Elizabeth Walshe. Several of them were described by fellow survivors as 'severely injured', having fallen into the wooden longboat then had other people land on them. No doubt cowed by the awful fate suffered by the young woman thrown overboard for crying,

A COURT FOR KING CHOLERA.

John Leech's cartoon *A Court for King Cholera* depicts the overcrowded – and filthy – living conditions typical of many inner cities of the time. Note the young chimney sweep and the woman picking through a rubbish heap while a child does a headstand in the pile. Small wonder so many chose to risk their lives emigrating overseas. (Punch, *25 September 1852*)

PUNCH, OR THE LONDON CHARIVARI.—JULY 3, 1853.

FATHER THAMES INTRODUCING HIS OFFSPRING TO THE FAIR CITY OF LONDON.
(A Design for a Fresco in the New Houses of Parliament.)

This cartoon *Father Thames introducing his offspring to the fair city of London. (A Design for a Fresco in the New Houses of Parliament.)* shows Diphtheria, Scrofula and Cholera crawling from a heavily polluted Thames which provided the drinking, cooking, and bathing water for thousands. (Punch, *3 July 1853*)

Interior of a Cottage in the Isle of Skye reveals a large but sparsely furnished and smoky rural home, with barefoot children watching a cooking pot as it dangles over an open fire. (Illustrated London News, *1853*)

Irish Emigrants Leaving Home – The Priest's Blessing was a familiar scene to many. Printed above the headline "THE DEPOPULATION OF IRELAND", many people were concerned that soon there would be almost no-one left there. (Illustrated London News, *10 May 1851*)

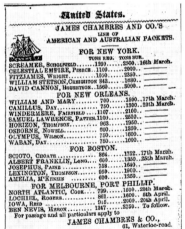

The somewhat misleading advert for the smaller-than-listed *William and Mary* does not – unlike the other vessels shown – include the name of the ship's captain, in this case the callous and cowardly Timothy R. Stinson. (Liverpool Mercury, *15 March 1853. Image © THE BRITISH LIBRARY BOARD. ALL RIGHTS RESERVED. Image reproduced with kind permission of The British Newspaper Archive www.britishnewspaperarchive.co.uk)*

If you didn't want your luggage stolen, you had to sit on it – and even then it might still be taken. The weak, tired, and unwary often lost all their possessions while waiting to board their chosen vessel. *Emigrants arrival at Cork. – A Scene on the Quay.* (Illustrated London News, *10 May 1851*)

Image of *William and Mary* from *Lotgevallen van den heer O. H. Bonnema*, 1853, used with kind permission of Collectie Tresoar. This is the only known image remaining of the ship.

This illustration of the *Cabin of 'The Madagascar,' and female emigrants* shows a spacious, clean, and relatively well-lit area below deck. Those travelling on the *William and Mary* would have benefitted from such a well-ordered ship. (*Illustrated London News, 12 March 1853*)

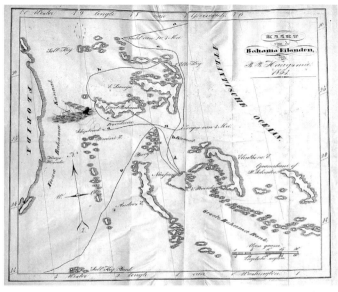

Map showing the doomed vessel's route through the Bahamas from *Lotgevallen van den heer O. H. Bonnema,* 1853. (*Image used with kind permission of Collectie Tresoar*)

View from Fort Fincastle, across Nassau and out to sea, from *The Isles of Summer* by C. Ives (1880). The survivors roamed these streets while they awaited suitable transport to New Orleans, and were greatly impressed by the kindness and generosity of the local people.

This view from high ground at the back of Nassau shows the magnificent houses and lush foliage of the island. (*The Isles of Summer* by C. Ives, 1880). (*Images used with kind permission of Pennymead.com*)

Johannes (John) Tuininga was 40 when he had to assist with pumping water from the wreck. An optimistic man despite the loss of two young children during the voyage, he cherished a fork discarded by a despondent friend and used it for the rest of his life. He had no time for the squabbles of the Frisian party and settled elsewhere with his family.

Trijntje Albers de Haan (Catherine Tuininga), a year younger than her husband, regretted the loss of her bag of keepsakes during the chaos of the rescue, particularly since it contained mementoes of the son and daughter lost on the voyage.

Jan (John) Tuininga was 16 when the ship wrecked. He, his parents and his surviving sisters went on to live long lives in America. (*All Tuininga images used with kind permission of Christopher Lindstrom*)

Sake Kooistra (Silas Coster), shown here shortly before his lingering death in the American Civil War, is remembered as a hero even now, over 150 years later. A fellow soldier said at the time of Silas's death at Gettysburg, 'No braver soldier ever lived or died'.

Sjoerd (Bekins) Bekius was 23 when he made it off the *William and Mary*. He went on to have a large and successful family.

Pictured here with his pipe, Sjoerd prospered in America, eventually dying aged 76 in Michigan. (*Both images used with kind permission of Ann Bekins*)

Beitske (Betsey) Gartner née Graafsma was 8 years old when she survived the shipwreck. Seen here in the 1890s seated amidst her family and beside her bearded husband, Adam, she went on to have over 200 descendants – equivalent to the *William and Mary*'s passenger list. (*Image used with kind permission of Joan McWhirter*)

Arjen Westerhuis (Aaron Westerhouse) and his wife survived the journey along with four of their five children and successfully settled in La Crosse County, Wisconsin. (*All Westerhouse images used with kind permission of Kim Frank*)

Hanne Westerhuis (Henry Westerhouse) was 11 when he survived the shipwreck. Pictured here in his Union uniform, he was one of many survivors who went on to fight in the American Civil War eight years later.

Tintypes took a while to expose, revealing every movement during a pose – including this horse's nodding head. As shown here, Henry served in the cavalry. His ease around horses would unfortunately lead to his demise forty years later.

A brave man, Henry is pictured here wearing a medal from the Grand Army of the Republic (G.A.R.), an organisation for Union Army veterans he was heavily involved with.

* * * PAINTED BY JOHN ABSOLON.

I'm very graceful and touching composition which we engrave, is one of the most attractive pieces in the "Winter Exhibition of Sketches and

Mary, the moon is sleeping on thy grave,
And on the turf thy lover said is kneel ng.

The artist represents the object of this passionate appeal, as rising spirit from the grave, and looking down in pity upon the bereaved

Mortality was high during the 1850s but despite early deaths being relatively commonplace it is clear each loss was keenly felt by those left behind. The fourteen who died during the voyage and the unknown two or three who perished as the captain and crew escaped the wreck were grieved for and remembered despite there being no grave for them but the open sea. (*Illustration from a painting by John Absolon, Illustrated London News, 2 April 1853*) there is little mention of them in accounts – but this may be in part because of the distraction provided by the men who began to fight amongst themselves.

Roorda, the youngest of the three Frisians to have escaped the shipwreck, sat with 26-year-old Ulbe Bergsma and Oene Wagenaar, 35, and listened in horror to the English-speakers around him. He had picked up a lot of the language in his time travelling across England and then also on the ship, which the other survivors appear to have been unaware of. They 'talked among themselves about throwing us three Frisians overboard and into the sea, to lighten the boat a little. As we had not treated them in the least harshly or surlily, this murderous attack aimed at us left us greatly shocked and constantly on our guard.'

It was as well that they were. The men on the longboat had already proven themselves willing to sacrifice others in order to increase their own chances of survival, using the hatchet on people they had been living alongside cordially for the previous six or seven weeks and throwing one woman overboard. Having been directly responsible for the deaths of fellow travellers already and with no guarantee of their own survival, the inhibitions usual in polite society were well and truly gone, as Roorda was about to discover.

[O]ne time they threw me on to the floor of the boat and held me down with their hands and feet, which made me soaking wet and it was only with the greatest effort and taking many rough blows that I managed to free myself and get back on my feet. They gave Ulbe Bergsma a frightful blow to the head, but as soon as we had drawn our knives and threatened to run through the first one who dared to touch us or throw us overboard, which we were well prepared to do, they stopped mistreating us, because it was clear that they were greatly afraid of our knives and possessed little fortitude. We returned once again to baling [*sic*] out water incessantly, in order to save our lives, with a knife in the other hand, while the sailors rowed, in the hope of reaching the quayside of Florida in the evening or at night.

Scotsman Ebenezer Miller was raging for other reasons and justifiably so.

The ship left the Mersey with her longboat unfit for sea, being neither caulked nor pitched, after being inspected by the government agent ... [F]our seamen being placed in [the lifeboat], who kept it a good way from the ship and two others being stationed at the line, to prevent any person from attempting to get on board of it ... these men were kept employed all the night and morning instead of assisting in getting the longboat made fit for sea and using other endeavours, such as in the construction of rafts, to save the lives of the people. Had it not been for the exertions of the other part of the crew, assisted by a number of the passengers, the longboat would never have floated even so much as half an hour on the water. As it was, it took four persons constantly bailing to keep the water down.

The sea was still rough, every knock and tip more obvious to the longboat's passengers than it had been on the much larger *William and Mary*, but at least there was daylight now. Those not bailing out the water flooding the bottom of the boat rowed, dipping the oars in and out of the waves, depending on the others to tell them which direction they ought to go in as they faced back towards the wreck. As Miller later said, 'We then followed the captain's boat, which we occasionally got a glimpse of in the distance, as we thought by this means the sooner to reach land, he being supposed to be the best acquainted with these parts.'

Miller, like so many of those on board, had a family to think of, but his was unconventional to say the least. The 26-year-old was something of a go-getter, an industrious young man with his own flax-dressing business who lived with his mother and father in Dundee along with his elder sister, Jean, and two small children whose origins are shrouded in mystery. According to a recent census, seven-year-old Ann Davidson and her brother Ebenezer, five, had been adopted by bachelor Ebenezer Miller. Born in Newport on the far-away Isle of Wight, off the south coast of England, their mother Dilminie Davidson had died of a fever in the barracks there when her son was about 18 months old. Her husband, Robert, was a private in the 42nd Regiment, possibly from the east of Scotland. Why this little boy shared a name with a seemingly unrelated single man in the port of Dundee who then adopted him and his sister is unknown. High mortality rates and long working hours meant children were often raised by people other than their parents, but these generally weren't single men. But whatever the children's history, they were family now and Ebenezer's instinct for self-preservation would help save him.

Meanwhile on the lifeboat, only a short time after they abandoned the wreck of the *William and Mary*, the situation was growing desperate. As the *Freeman's Journal* of 31 May 1853 would later report, 'One of the sailors, named John Best, says that the boat in which he was [was] so crowded that they were seriously debating the propriety of drawing lots to see who should go overboard, as it was feared that the boat would be swamped.' Drawing lots among survivors was an old custom and for all that it was meant to be a fair way of choosing who survived, it was often carefully rigged to ensure the youngest, weakest or least popular person was chosen. No doubt 17-year-old Nova Scotian John Best was aware of this and perhaps that is why this stuck so clearly in his mind.

They had taken a box of bread and a small can of water, containing at most three gallons, with them when they fled. Even with their sail assisting them in their journey towards the coast of Florida, rowing after a night of no sleep and plenty of hard work would have been thirsty work. But a few hours later, there was hope.

Stinson described how at midday, 'a bark bore in sight, bound up the Gulf, which proved to be an English vessel'. Unfortunately for the captain and the eight crewmen packed in beside him, 'The lifeboat in which I was [was] too far leeward to be seen by the bark, but she fortunately fell in with the longboat, containing the passengers and some of the crew and picked them up.' Roorda, Miller and the others were saved.

[A]t 12 o'clock in the afternoon we caught sight of a ship, we tried to row towards it, which with the greatest effort and difficulty, combined with the fact that we had to head into the wind and the sea was so hollow that several times our boat almost stood upright, sometimes with the front and at other times with the back end resting on a wave, or as if hidden between two waves which rose up around us like mountains. From the deck of the ship nobody could detect us, but luckily there happened to be sailors up in the masts who discovered our boat and saw how we were expending every effort to approach them; they immediately gave notice to the captain, who immediately ordered the yards to be retracted, so that the vessel came to lie still and we could reach it with ease; one can understand how this brought us the utmost happiness.

On arriving at the ship, the crew let down a ladder that we climbed up and so reached safety, being received with the greatest love and courtesy. Very soon questions were exchanged on both sides between the crew and ourselves, whereby we learned that the ship on which we found ourselves was named the *Pollux*, captain Mac. Entijre [McIntyre], coming from New Orleans and destined for Liverpool and that had we been a quarter of an hour later, they would not have been able to see us and this chance of rescue would have been lost to us – this salvation, unforgettable to me, took place … between 12 and 1 o'clock in the afternoon.

We had spent only a few moments on the *Pollux* when we were provided with food and drink, which we needed as greatly as rest, as we had consumed nothing since 5 o'clock on the previous afternoon, being the usual suppertime on the *William and Mary* and had been working hard non-stop with an extraordinary effort, both by pumping the abandoned ship and by baling [*sic*] out the boat. During the course of the afternoon Captain McIntyre appealed to two ships which were bound for New York, with a request to take us in, but their captains wanted nothing to do with it and sailed on, meanwhile we begged and implored the captain to try to save those who were left behind on our previous ship, all the more because we could still see its masts until 6 o'clock in the evening, the captain promised us that he would see in the evening if such a thing was possible, which calmed us a little in respect of their rescue, because we still feared that the ship could sink or be destroyed at any moment and help would therefore come too late; yet that evening the *Pollux* sailed on, the captain said that he did not dare to come so close to the rocks to save those left behind on the *William and Mary*, we could now do no more than commend them to the good God and the following morning we were already so far distant that we could no longer see anything of the ship.

On the first day we were shown our accommodation below the deck with the sailors of the crew, but the next day this was changed and not for the better for us, because from then on we were not allowed to be anywhere but on deck under the open sky, the pump was taken out of the water tank and the entire crew was put on rations, for although they had brought plenty of provisions for themselves, it was seen as a matter of thrift and negotiation, because the personnel was doubled by our 27 castaways.

They could have fared a lot worse, as survivors of a shipwreck in the same area the previous year had discovered. '[A]fter exerting every effort to preserve the vessel from entire destruction, it was deemed prudent to order the hands to take to the boats. The crew, with Mr. Wallace, the passenger, put off in the long-boat and gig and hovered about at a safe distance. Exposed as the unfortunate men were to a powerful sun, their sufferings from thirst became most intense and as days passed by without there seeming the least chance of being observed, a terrible fate appeared to await them all … [Finally they were rescued by another vessel but food soon ran out.] Some rats were caught on board and, being cooked, were devoured with much relish. The contents of the grease pot were also consumed and, indeed, anything that could sustain life.' (*York Herald*, 9 October 1852)

Back on the lifeboat, there were no rats for the men to consume when the bread ran out. They carried on rowing west for America, keeping a lookout for sails or the stinking thick black smoke of a steamer and one hour later they spotted something.

Captain Stinson later reported that, 'At 1 o'clock a brig hove in sight, which proved to be the Reuben Carver, Rockland, Maine, Captain Cobb, bound from Sagua la Grande to New York. She was, at the time we boarded her under close-reefed foretopsail and two-reefed mainsail.' As luck would have it, the ship was from Captain Stinson and many of his crewmen's home state and, unlike the *Pollux*, bound for an American port. Unfortunately for the approximately 175 men, women and children Stinson had abandoned early that morning, the *Reuben Carver* did not come back for them, but then why would Captain Cobb do so if his fellow captain had told him he had witnessed the *William and Mary* sink beneath the waves six hours earlier?

Luck smiled on the errant captain and his crew again when they crossed paths with another Maine ship, the barque *Oneco*, six days later. The *Reuben Carver*, like the Liverpool-bound *Pollux*, was running out of provisions far more quickly than Captain Cobb had expected when he first left port, but those on board the passing barque took sympathy on them and, according to 31 May 1853's *Dublin Evening Packet and Correspondent*, 'generously supplied them with all they wanted'.

The newspaper also gave Stinson the opportunity to defend his rescuer,

As Captain Cobb's conduct in not looking after the sinking vessel has been censured in some quarters, I desire to state here that it would have been perfectly impossible to have beat his vessel against the wind, sea and Gulf Stream, to reach the *William and Mary*, even if she had been afloat which it would have been foolish to suppose. I would take the present opportunity of returning my thanks to Capt. Cobb and his lady for their kindness and hospitality to myself and those who were saved with me. They did everything in their power to render us comfortable.

Crewman Stephen Perrington echoed this praise, 'I have only to say that we received every kindness and attention from the captain, his wife and crew [that they] could render us.'

As Stinson and the majority of his crew sailed for the safety of the Atlantic Dock in Brooklyn, New York with plentiful food, drink and sympathy, Roorda and those rescued from the longboat were struggling on the cold wet decks of the *Pollux* as they sailed back east across the Atlantic.

[A]t night we lay on top of the cable ropes, which caused us great pain and discomfort and whenever it rained we were soon soaked through, because we had nothing for cover other than a sail that the rain quickly penetrated while the cold and wind also tested us severely, whereas by day we suffered greatly from a sometimes unbearable heat, to crown it all my clogs had been broken beyond repair when I jumped into the boat, so that I had to walk about in stockings under which I had put a couple of old scraps of sail, as a result of which I always had wet feet for at least half the day, as my feet got thoroughly wet in the morning when the deck was cleaned.

He later wrote of how the monotony of the voyage was broken by the appearance on board of a large seabird with a wingspan of five feet and 'very strong' beak and legs. Despite the helmsman trying to scare it away with a lump of coal one of the sailors managed to keep it as a pet for a week. There is no mention of them using it for food, which may have proved the wrong decision.

Our life on the ship became even more unpleasant meantime, on May 9th and the two following days it was still and we had a headwind, which increased the unpleasant disposition of the sailors towards us, when we asked them for a dish or plate to have our food on, we had to listen to the worst abuse from them and this was truly no surprise, as we, though we were dreadfully hungry, now had to endure our hunger and thirst, while they would otherwise have had a surplus; the result of this was that the sailors and steersmen began to consider on May 12th that if the calm [remained] for some time, it might be advisable to try to reach the Azores and set us down there, the more so because ships frequently arrived there that were bound for all parts of the earth, by which we would probably soon find an opportunity to return to Europe, but the wind that later came, being almost always favourable, was the reason that they did not put this plan into effect.

For the next two days the calm continued, by which the crew's dissatisfaction and unpleasant treatment of us worsened, so that they hardly left us in peace for a moment and our situation became almost unbearable, in addition to which it was often and in particular on May 16th, so dreadfully warm that it was almost impossible to walk unshod on the planks of the deck; the heat almost scorched my feet, whilst on other days it could be so cold that we had to use all the scarce means at our disposal to gain some warmth and frequently stood trembling from the cold. My two Frisian fellows had the additional misfortune on May 25th of losing their shirts, having hung them on a rope to be washed clean by the waves, when the water threw them against a chain so that they could not get them off again and the shirts were torn to shreds, because of which they were required to do without the items of clothing we needed for our arrival in England.

Eventually the weather improved, allowing the *Pollux* to continue, wind filling the sails and rushing the ship across the Atlantic. In addition, it rained for a full morning, washing the salt from their skin and allowing the sailors to catch 'a good portion of fresh water, which the captain allowed them to keep for their own use, moreover allowing them to share out the usual rations; this, combined with the wind remaining favourable, made the disposition of the team towards us much more benevolent and better and they left us alone'.

Back in New York, a city teeming with the newly arrived and the people who made a living off them, Stinson and his crew dispersed. The first mate left for Boston, the second mate immediately shipped out on another vessel and the rest scattered like rats before a terrier. The captain reported the *William and Mary* as lost before his eyes, devastating those awaiting friends and relatives who were on the ship, then fled far from the coast, into the Midwest. The eight crewmen who had been in the lifeboat with him joined other crews or otherwise made themselves scarce – but not before talking to journalists about their awful experience.

The *Morning Post* of 30 May 1853 quoted the *New York Daily Times*, saying:

These poor people, numbering in all upwards of 200, were wending their way to this country in search of home and its comforts, bringing with them all their worldly possessions. Their career has met an untimely and awful check. As before stated, the names of none of them has transpired, nor, so far as we can learn, was there any record of the number received on board the barque ... The screams and agonised appeals for aid from the decks of the ill-fated barque still linger upon the ear of the few survivors. We conversed yesterday with an intelligent seaman, a Dane, who was one of the nine persons picked up by the *Reuben Carver* and brought to this port and gathered from him the particulars of some of the scenes on board the vessel. He was impressed with a feeling sense of the horrors of the calamity and desired never to witness such another scene. The yells of the unfortunate wretches who were left to perish are described as unearthly. Irish, Dutch, German, each in his own vernacular, joined in imploring help from quarters where none was to be obtained. Not a spar, we are credibly informed, was made loose; not a mast was cut away; not a raft was constructed; the boats were swamped and the vessel was sinking. Of those on board, not less than one hundred and seventy persons must have met a certain death. A terrible loss of life is undoubtedly the result of this calamity and the long catalogue of disasters receives a melancholy addition. Further accounts from the owners and the captain, will be awaited with great interest.

Newspapers around the world, including the Irish *Freeman's Journal* of 31 May 1853, were – along with many individuals – horrified by Stinson's haste to get away.

One of the sailors is of opinion that some of the passengers may have formed a raft and saved themselves upon it. This he [Capt. Stinson] considers not at all improbable, as there were two or three sailors left behind on the vessel and these, he believes, would have devised some such means of saving themselves and some of the passengers ... Could there be a more convincing proof of the cowardice or insensibility of Captain Stinson? If safety by means of a raft was open to the doomed emigrants, with the aid of two or three sailors, how much greater the chances of safety if the captain and his crew had clung to the ship and exerted themselves to provide the means of escape. If the raft was 'not at all improbable,' why did he not hover around the abandoned ship and wait to know the result, instead of rowing away as fast as oars could take him and then administering comfort on 'the opinion of one of the sailors'!

Shipwrecks were so common as to be almost unremarkable, meriting in some cases only a brief mention in the newspapers indicating that a vessel had not been seen in some months despite travelling in a major shipping route, or had not reached its destination. But Stinson's apparent lack of gallantry and courage – and humanity – appalled even the most cynical, hardened hack. The shipwreck of the troopship HMS *Birkenhead*, where 450 drowned or were eaten by great white sharks off the coast of South Africa having first sent the women and children off to safety in lifeboats, had only happened fifteen months previously and was still fresh in people's minds. This disaster sparked the procedure known as the 'Birkenhead drill' where those deemed the weakest on board – women and children – were evacuated before anyone else, although this had its own hierarchy following race, nationality and – that great obsession of the Victorians – class. Stinson's callous abandonment of his vessel and the families on board in the shark filled waters of the Bahamas was the total opposite of the aspirational Victorian standard of 'women and children first'.

The *New York Times* of 18 May 1853 was outspoken in its outrage, suspicious of Stinson and his brief account of the tragedy and described it as 'imperfectly set before the public'. They went on to castigate him in detail, reproaching the captain for his apparent silence regarding the reported death of over 170 emigrants who entrusted their lives to his care. Stinson's 'sudden disappearance' when people and papers all over the world wanted answers served to arouse their suspicions too.

It appears, from all the accounts we are able to gather, that the *William and Mary*, loaded with upward of two hundred emigrant passengers, in addition to a heavy cargo of iron, sailed from Liverpool for New-Orleans and while passing the Bahamas, struck a sunken reef and sunk in less than twelve hours afterward. Out of the whole number of passengers on board the vessel, barely thirty escaped. ... The emigrants, totally unskilled in the management of vessels, were permitted to crowd into the boats in such numbers as to break them away from the davits, thus destroying the slender hope of relief afforded by the ordinary appointments of the ship. None of the masts, spars, deck-timbers or other life-saving materials, were cast loose. The water gained rapidly in the hold, the ship became ungovernable, went to pieces and one hundred and seventy souls were lost. The result is a frightful chapter to be added to the record of the past month and the impression cannot but prevail that in this case, as in so many others, the cause is traceable to culpable negligence and carelessness. Had the officers in charge kept a bright watch for dangers, there is nothing to indicate that the reef might not have been avoided; had the Captain taken more effective measures for the preservation of his passengers and his papers, the loss would have been less serious. And, finally, the silence and speedy exodus of Captain STINSON argues that there is little to be offered in extenuation. That a sea-captain should coldly report that his vessel had 'gone down.' and 'it is supposed that all on board perished,' is altogether too systematic and provokes disagreeable emotions. It was at least due to the public that a statement duly authenticated by the survivors, should have been prepared and published by the Master, before he found it convenient to leave New-York for his home in Bowdoinham. If there is a reason for this silence, or an explanation for this seeming carelessness, the public will be glad to hear it.

Such a public attack on his character and actions would have been shocking to Stinson, the shipowners and all who knew them. At this point, Stinson and the crew of the lifeboat had been back in the US – even if just briefly – for several days. The *New York Tribune* of the same day was also deeply suspicious of Stinson's account.

The details of the shipwreck … are of such a nature as to require special remark. We hear of some two hundred people who went down with her, but that the *Captain and crew* escaped in a boat. We do not wish to condemn the Captain. To arrive at the command of a ship requires tedious years of toil, exposure and danger and the place gained is full of technical responsibilities and anxieties. But any one who has made a voyage must have observed the spontaneous regard and respect which are paid by the passengers to the commander, especially on the part of the feminine portion of the company … [I]t is expected the Captain's devotion and heroism are equal to every emergency. Each person believes, that in case of wreck, the Captain will be the last to leave his vessel. That, he at least will die with or even without his old guard at his Waterloo. Thus is he the type of courage, of that quality which is most admired. We were surprised therefore to learn that Capt. Stinson and his crew had escaped, while some two hundred persons entrusted to his care, were lost ... we should like, in deference to the public, to have a little light on the subject; of how it was that captain, officers and crew, could be saved, but so few of the passengers? We simply ask for information, for our idea of a captain's duty has been, that he should think most of his passengers and least of himself. Was this the case in question?

Clearly not.

Another major American paper took him to task, questioning the accuracy of the location given for the wreck and saying:

The Boston Journal suspects that there are errors in Capt. Stinson's account of the loss of his vessel, with fearful destruction of human life, or that there was mismanagement at the time of that occurrence ... According to [Stinson's] statement the ship struck on a rock on the northern part of the Great Bahama Bank ... At that time the Great Isaac hove E.S.E., seven miles distant ... [I]t is singular that, with a strong breeze, instead of being anchored, the ship was not kept under way through the night and every effort made to get farther on the bank into shoal water, where the chances of all on board being saved would have been infinitely greater than while the ship remained in ten fathoms of water.

People were clamouring for further information but after releasing a second statement with a few more details included regarding the weather and the journey in general (and no mention of the ship going down before his eyes as he escaped in the lifeboat, as he had initially stated), Stinson remained silent, with rumours swirling through the media of him escaping to Australia to avoid the – as they saw it – wholly justifiable censure of his actions in the press.

Perhaps he and the owners were hoping that if they just kept quiet subsequent news would fill the papers and distract the journalists from seeking further, possibly damning, information. Perhaps they were right and this would have happened, leaving Stinson and the owners of the *William and Mary* to get on with their lives and deal with their financial losses in private.

But then the *Pollux* arrived in England and reports from Roorda and Miller stimulated fresh interest in the story. Roorda released an account of the experience and the relief of returning to dry land.

In the afternoon of June 1st we saw the Irish coast; one can imagine what a tremendous happiness this aroused in us, our joy was unbounded when we saw a great number of large and small ships around us, fishermen came on board trying to sell fish to the crew, which however was not made use of.

The next day we had a headwind at first and later it became dead calm, in the afternoon we again saw land and a very notable mass of ships, again fishermen came on board our ship to peddle their catch to us, at which, as the sailors had no money, an exchange took place between them and the fishermen, our crew now traded fish for tobacco, while the captain bought some with meat. The fishermen seemed to be very satisfied with this trade, the tobacco in particular was of great value to them, because this was so expensive in England and cost at least two and a half guilders a pound.

The three days after this the wind changed constantly, so that we could only make very little progress, this disappointment of our hopes to be able to reach Liverpool very quickly again was meanwhile somewhat compensated by the fact that on the 4th we each received a piece of the fish from the captain that he had bought two days ago, this was a real feast for our hungry bellies.

In the afternoon of the 5th the wind was very favourable for us, so that we were able to head towards our destination at great speed, our ship sailed with such great progress that in the evening we drew alongside a propeller steamship, being the same one in which we later travelled to Rotterdam, which in the morning had steamed past us, though we then had to watch it pull out ahead of us because we had to wait for a pilot to come on board. At 3 o'clock in the afternoon the captain gave the sign with the flags, that he wished for that steamship to come over to us that same evening, in order to take us to the city, which I was told was at a distance of 20 hours from Liverpool; at 9 o'clock in the evening the boat came to us, immediately took the ship on tow and brought us early the following morning to the river by Liverpool and so I saw before me for the second time this great trading city, never having thought, when I left it ten weeks earlier, that I would see it again, so soon and bereft of everything.

After spending ten weeks at sea, Roorda and his companions were hungry, thirsty, exhausted, sunburnt and traumatised but grateful to be alive. They were also completely penniless in a city full of other would-be travellers, just as impoverished and destitute. Despite this, as Roorda later wrote, people were kind towards them.

Early in the morning of the 6th of June custom agents came aboard to check the baggage of the crew for tobacco. Unfortunately for them no tobacco was found. The sailors re-packed their baggage and left the ship. We did not have the opportunity to thank the captain for his hospitality since he had left the ship the previous night. I was deeply ashamed to leave the ship in socks so that my 2 Friesian friends decided to buy me a pair. A little later Ulbe Bergsma arrived with a pair of shoes. Then we left the ship that had been like a guardian angel to us in fearful days. We had been through a lot and had suffered much. Words cannot express my feelings, so happy, so grateful I was standing again on the same quay after so many weeks on the ocean. We returned to the same inn where we had been before; here Ulbe Bergsma had borrowed money to buy shoes for me. The friendly German owners had burst into tears when they heard of the shipwreck and did not know if any others survived. They immediately supplied us with clothing and made arrangements so that we could refresh ourselves. After that a delicious hot meal was ready for us.

I wrote home at once and told them I would return home as soon as possible. In Liverpool we saw various Dutch ships and I met a Frisian friend I had not seen for years. Together we saw a great deal of Liverpool which made my stay here more agreeable. We were advised to approach the insurance company of the William & Mary to complain and ask for a return of part of our fare since we had not arrived at our destination. We each received 30 guildres. With this we could pay the inn for our clothing and our stay. We were also directed by the insurance company to go to the Dutch consulate where we were promised that they would pay our travel costs to our own Netherlands ... We thanked God that he spared us and that he had brought us safely back to our fatherland. Our thoughts were constantly with those who had remained in the William & Mary and we hoped that God had treated them humanely.

They would soon find out.

Chapter Nine

Now commenced a scene impossible to describe, for when the boat was cut adrift it was found that some of those who were in the boat had left their wives, some their fathers and mothers and some their brothers and sisters – and these stood weeping and tearing their hair and calling upon them to come back again, saying, 'Let us all die together!' … We were now in a most painful condition, without a boat, without any one who knew where we were, or who could direct us what to do. However we had a little council together and it was agreed that we should slip the cable and try and make the land which we had passed the previous day. The first thing, however, that we did was to set the pumps going again, they having stopped during the time that the long boat was being lowered. We let slip the cable and away we drifted. We now tried to make sail, but we soon found out that it was no easy thing, for during the night the braces both fore and aft had been cut away, also the head stays. We were then entirely at the mercy of the winds and waves and we drifted we know not where.

(Joseph Brooks, passenger)

On the Wreck, 4–5 May

Back on the stricken *William and Mary*, 175 desperate men, women and children were in peril and the two crewmen remaining on the ship were not of a mind to help. William Ward and Samuel Harris had been unpopular with the captain – there were rumours of thieving – and they, along with the cook sacked a few weeks prior, had been refused entry to the boats. Captain Stinson had even threatened to slit their throats if they attempted to come aboard. They would later say that they had 'refused to quit the ship and abandon the helpless and unfortunate passengers' and claim they 'tried to get the ship under weigh, in order, if possible, to reach the land and run the ship ashore, but the passengers could render very little assistance in working the ships [*sic*] and therefore [we] were unable to do so. Had not the captain and crew deserted the ship, it is [our conviction]

that the ship might have been run ashore' (*Nassau Guardian*, 14 May 1853).
As Shakespeare wrote in *The Merchant of Venice*, 'Ships are but boards,
sailors but men'. Now, instead of taking charge of the situation and the ship,
one of them proclaimed himself captain and they both proceeded to help
themselves to the contents of one of the drowned German's casks of alcohol.
Neither seems to have been a pleasant drunk and Haagsma, a teetotaller,
later wrote, 'they had lost their common sense. They had ... partaken freely
of that liquor, which turns a person into a beast.' But the passengers had not
given up all hope as yet.

One of the Frisians, 43-year-old Sjoerd Tjalsma, had previously worked
as a skipper. Still grieving the loss of his eldest son, Lyckle, on board a
few weeks earlier, he nonetheless managed to put his experience to good
use, along with 45-year-old Scotsman John Brown, a civil engineer who'd
worked for the Navy. Everyone was exhausted, worn out from a night of
terror if not from working the pump, but despite their suffering they carried
on. If they didn't, they would die.

The group divided into those praying for salvation and those pumping
water from the hold. Dr van der Veer had been pumping but his skills as a
doctor soon meant he was required elsewhere. Susannah Diamond, 19, had
been emigrating with her husband, John, baby Margaret and the rest of her
family from the pits of Durham in the north of England to the mining area
around St Louis. She was visibly pregnant with their second child when the
ship was wrecked and devastated when her husband left her behind, making
his escape in a panicked rush on the leaky longboat. As Joseph Brooks
described it, 'A singular occurrence happened here. One of the women,
whose husband was in the boat, was so enraged at his cowardly conduct that
she actually took off her wedding ring and threw it after him, muttering
something ... which I could not understand.' She wept and wailed ... and
went into an early labour.

The devout Christians among the Frisian group no doubt recalled the
line in Genesis that says, 'In sorrow thou shalt bring forth children'. It
was certainly true for poor Susannah. Childbirth is a risky process even
under the cleanest, safest conditions. To deliver a child on a sinking ship
after spending six weeks at sea (and therefore not being in a particularly
hygienic place anyway) was a terrifying prospect. Dr van der Veer assisted

an experienced midwife travelling with the Bonnema party to care for Susannah. Frisian midwives were trained and operated under licence within their communities. Despite the language barrier, Susannah was in the best hands possible.

Susannah had married John Diamond in the coastal town of Hartlepool, around the time she turned 18, while around five months pregnant with Margaret. They were approaching their second wedding anniversary when they boarded the *William and Mary* with her family, seeking a new life in the sun. Many Victorians had a somewhat business-like concept of marriage, as revealed in the *Coventry Herald* of 3 June 1853,

> A man gets a wife to look after his affairs and assist him in his journey through life; to educate and prepare his children for a proper station in life and not to dissipate his property. The husband's interest should be the wife's care and her greatest ambition to carry her no further than his welfare or happiness, together with that of her children. This should be her sole aim and the theatre of her exploits, in the bosom of her family …

Romance may not have been the main reason for their nuptials, but whatever their relationship was like, to have been abandoned like this was a gross betrayal of Susannah's trust in her husband. She also had no idea of whether he was alive or dead and this worry added to her fears as she readied herself to deliver their baby.

Elsewhere on the ship, 39-year-old Trijntje de Haan was mourning the loss of her children Antje and Gerrit earlier in the journey and afraid for the lives of the rest of her family. Her husband, Johannes Tuininga, 40, was one of the team of men pumping water from the hold and she had three children to comfort and keep out of harm's way. Her descendant later said, 'Through all my grandmother's grief and weakness she held tight in her hand a bag containing articles she valued. [Along with] her head dress … were silver spoons, laces, some trinkets and keepsakes and, most precious of all, the clothing of her dead children.'

The weather was foul, lashing those on deck with rain, soaking their hair and clothing and adding to the general misery. A young Frisian man,

23-year-old Jan Janzen, braved the weather, climbing slippery ropes and spars in order to attach the distress flag in a place where passing vessels could actually see it. He looked for sails or land or any signs of salvation but there were none to be found. Waves slapped the sides of the ship, splashing over the men at the pumps and still the water rose.

While some men pumped and other people prayed, some stranded passengers got busy elsewhere. Joseph Brooks later stated that 'About 12 o'clock it was proposed to make some rafts, hoping thereby to save some by that means if the ship went down before assistance could come to us. We made two rafts, capable of holding fifty persons each.' Haagsma was more pessimistic, saying, '[We] considered it to be wise, under the circumstances, to make rafts on which we could spend our final moments, when the ship sank.'

This meant seventy-five people would have to find another mode of survival. Sometimes, depending on the temperature of the water, the currents and the kind of creatures lurking beneath the surface, shipwreck survivors would take turns holding onto the edge of a raft or piece of wreckage in order to maximise the number of people remaining alive. In the relatively warm and shallow waters of the Bahamas, however, this would have been inviting trouble.

Six months after the wreck of the *William and Mary*, an American bark, the *Hyperion*, sank off the coast of North Carolina. Only four crewmen survived and were eventually rescued after several days of 'almost continued submersion'. Their story was a harrowing one.

As the ship foundered the two mates and the seaman contrived to get hold of the aide of the forecastle house and the captain upon the piece of the top of the hatch house, five feet square. The night was very severe and it was only by holding on with all their strength that they escaped being washed off by the heavy seas which kept breaking over them. The captain saw nothing of the three men on the side of the forecastle.

… Captain Perkins found a more secure kind of raft in a portion of the top of the forecastle house. There was a hole through which the pipe of the stove passed through which he put his legs and which enabled him to keep his hold on the wood. In this position he was buffeted about by the ocean until Wednesday morning, the water being up to his armpits. The weather had but very little moderated; he suffered much from cold, thirst and severe cramps; death seemed to him inevitable; and, once or twice, so severe was his suffering and hopeless his chance of rescue, that he had an idea of casting himself off, but for a shark which kept dodging about the raft the whole two days, at times almost rubbing its sides against the timber....

Like their captain, [the other three] endured great suffering. The woodwork to which they clung and which afforded not the least hold beyond the grasping of the ends, was just and only sufficient to bear them up, for the sea flooded the part where they sat. However they did not despair. They buoyed up each other's spirits and tried to make light of their time in endeavouring to scare away two or three sharks which kept floundering about their frail and swamping craft.

The crew of the *William and Mary* had recently dropped the tiny body of four-year-old Rinske Westerhuis overboard as a burial at sea and several people had drowned or died of loss of blood and shock in the water nearby just hours before. As far as the sharks of the area were concerned, the sinking vessel was a prime source of food. It was simply not sensible to abandon the ship on rafts if there was any way at all of keeping the holed vessel afloat.

A few hours later, there was hope.

People were constantly scanning the horizon in search of help and Haagsma later recalled that they 'looked around to see if we could discover land or a ship here or there. Finally we saw a 3-master; but, alas, as happy as we were to see it appear, we were disappointed to see it disappear.' According to Joseph Brooks, 'At 5 in the afternoon we saw a ship and thought she was coming to us, but, like the Levite, she only looked on and passed by. Darkness was now gathering fast upon us and not one in the ship thought that we should see the morning.' This was possibly the *Pollux*, but the rough seas and treacherous rocks and reefs nearby meant it was too unsafe for the ship to approach the survivors without possibly wrecking themselves. As Captain Stinson should have known and perhaps had, this was no place for a ship.

Haagsma continued,

[E]vening approached, as the weather became more unfavorable. The scene became more dreadful as the storming elements were covered by the drape of the night, when the thunder rolled, the lightening [*sic*] flashed, the storm wind howled and the rain pelted down. The anxiety of the passengers was so great that many tied themselves to the raft with ropes, awaiting death there.

Siebren Wesselius was one of them.

The water rose higher, notwithstanding our pumping. Night came and our hope began to want. Death seemed inevitable. Everyone sought for ropes to tie to each other so they would die together. The storm accompanied with rain, thunder and lightning and although I too was united to my wife and children by means of a rope, I continually called upon Him. I thought of the words 'Call upon Me in the day of distress and I will help you and thou shalt honor Me.' I thought, the Lord can send deliverance, if we might only live to see the next day.

They weren't the only people to have hoped and prayed in the face of almost-certain death in this area of the West Atlantic. Captain Stinson's mishandling and desertion of the *William and Mary* wreck was a stark contrast to the similar wrecking of the much larger packet ship *Toronto* in the Bahamas two years earlier. Back then,

Captain Parker, discovering the fearful position they were placed in, ordered his men to cut away the masts. This step eased the ship for a time … She continued thumping on the rocks and Captain Parker, fearing she would break up, had the boats cleared, supplied with bread and water and launched. During the night the ship remained a fixture and at daybreak the following morning the sounding of the pumps showed there was no fewer than eighteen feet of water in the hold. The weather moderating, Captain Parker determined to remain by the wreck as long as it was practicable. All that day, next night and following day and not a sail bore in sight. Another mournful night was passed, the crew and passengers suffering intensely. The wreck sunk down on the reef and the decks, with the exception of the quarter-deck, were completely under water. The following morning the passengers were got into the boats and the crew and master followed, with the intention of proceeding to the Bahama Islands. Just, however, as the boats were shoving off, a vessel, which proved to be the Vandelia, was perceived making for the wreck. They held on and in the course of a short time she came up and took them all on board in perfect safety.

This was reported in the *Tralee Chronicle* on 8 February 1851 and may well have been read by some of the Irish passengers travelling on the *William and Mary*. Whether the report of the passengers' eventual salvation provided any kind of comfort to them is impossible to say.

Elsewhere on board, Susannah was in pain. Her baby was coming and there was little her family, Dr van der Veer or the midwife could do for her. The water was rising as torrential rain fell on deck and the storm forced ever more seawater into the hold. The *William and Mary* had been a shipwreck for an agonising 36 hours. Joseph Brooks and the rest of the men on deck 'were becoming very fatigued, having worked very hard at the pumps.' But Haagsma wasn't ready to die without a fight: 'We decided to sell our lives at the highest possible price and pumped on.'

Bekius was in despair. '[T]he thunder roared, the heavens covered with dark clouds and the bright flashes of lightning repeatedly lit up the dark nightly scene. Morning finally broke, but all hope for deliverance seemed vain; our sufferings had not yet come to an end, there still remained much suffering in store for us. The ship began to sink more and more, the crisis seemed to be at hand. But the saying that where the need is greatest deliverance is near proved to be true.'

Brooks was delighted when 'in the midst of our troubles daylight broke in upon us and about 4 ½ in the morning we saw land ahead of us about eight miles off'. The low-lying island was one of the Bahama group, many of which had very small populations. This was no busy coastline bustling with fishing boats and speedy clippers, but a generally peaceful paradise of palm trees and pale sand. They had somewhere to aim for in hopes of beaching the wreck but no-one to assist them. Then, according to the deeply religious Hendrik Jans Kas, 'Suddenly God caused the wind to die down and we had the finest weather in the world and the sea was as smooth as glass.' Wesselius was watching the horizon and 'when it began to dawn, we saw a sail, but it disappeared out of our sight. [Then a]bout eight o'clock we saw another ship ...'

As an emotional Bekius later reported, 'Then the fathers and their children dropped on their knees praying to God that this might prove to be their deliverer and this prayer was answered. The darkling twilight was transformed into light when we saw our deliverer draw near.' An equally relieved Haagsma wrote, 'Finally May 5 dawned, the day commemorating the Lord's ascension. And it was upon that day that we experienced His wise, invisible hand extended in a wonderful way. Namely, when we were filled with gratitude, as we saw land in the early morning and later a ship. Oh! how eagerly every eye was fixed upon the horizon from whence help was anticipated. And a few moments later you should have seen the tears of joy flow as the aforesaid ship turned toward us.'

While the ship sailed towards them across an azure blue sea, the sun warming the day and boosting their spirits still further, the emigrants were also thinking of the young woman and her pain. Susannah was in the final stages of labour, half-submerged in water and as her husband John travelled back towards Liverpool on the *Pollux* without her, their second child was born. Despite the support of her family and the Frisian doctor and midwife, the child only survived half an hour. That the child lived at all, considering he or she was premature and born into such a terrible situation, was little short of incredible.

As Haagsma put it, her plight 'greatly aroused everyone's pity'. Her parents, who were travelling with her, could sympathise, at least to an extent. They had lost their only son, Adam, when his big sister Susannah was six and her sister Isabella four. The Stewarts' son was 18 months old when he died of 'inflammation of the lungs' and although child mortality was high, he would have been greatly missed. Susannah, having already lost her daughter Margaret during the voyage, had now lost her husband and another child in quick succession. But the approach of this vessel meant she and the other 174 aboard the *William and Mary* might not lose their lives.

Chapter Ten

... daylight revealed our true situation. I need not describe to you, who have felt all the horrors of shipwreck, the anxious suspense of those long hours, when we did not know but that at the next instant we should be engulphed [sic] in the raging billows, which again and again spent their fury on our shattered hull, making every timber crack and yield in the unequal contest ... [Nearby we could see] a low chain of reefy islands; and still further west, the wooded shores of the island of Abaco ... we could see the light sails of the wreckers pushing boldly forth to sea. Soon a little fleet of the egg-shell craft, in which the wreckers tempt the waves, hovered round about our dismantled vessel, like wolves over the carcass of a buffalo. Many of them boarded us and, contrary to the opinion generally received of this class of men, exhibited much willingness in lending assistance. With their aid, in less than three hours the whole command, with most of the personal baggage, was safely landed on Fowl Cay. Though saved from the perils of the deep, we found ourselves on a ragged mass of coral rock, without water or food and entirely dependent for provision on what might be saved from the ship; for the near island of Abaco is inhabited only by these poor wreckers, who live on fish and a few of the tropical fruits. In a few days, however, to collect a good supply of provisions; and, except in the particular of water, which was scanty, lived very well on our newly populated island.

(Account of another shipwreck, *Morning Post*, 1 December 1847)

At Sea, Thursday 5 May

The vessel now approaching the stricken *William and Mary* was a wrecking schooner called the *Oracle*. Captained by 33-year-old Robert 'Amphibian' Sands – so-called because of his abilities as a swimmer – the vessel was a godsend to the approximately 175 desperate individuals clinging to life on the wreck, who, as the son of survivor Jan Tuininga later wrote, 'were nearly dead from disease, thirst and starvation'.

The *Oracle* came alongside and Captain Sands immediately called for the women and children to come aboard. A father of five, with a pregnant wife of his own at home, the family man was keen to send what were seen as the more vulnerable passengers to safety first. At less than a twelfth of the size, the 41-ton vessel was dwarfed by the emigrant ship and could only safely carry some of the survivors at one time. The wreckers moved with haste and assurance, assisting the emotional emigrants onto their boat and paying special attention to the devastated Susannah Diamond. As John Gregory, the Governor of the Bahamas, later wrote to the British Government:

Robert Sands (a native of the Bahama Islands and a shining example of practical humanity) caught a glimpse of the distressed ship and instantly bore down upon her. Your Grace will not require me to describe the feelings of this mass of human beings crowded together on the quarter deck of a ship within a few hours of sinking when our Bahamsan [*sic*] wrecker hurried to their relief. Capt. Sands to his honour I lay it, never thought of salvage but at once took off women and children – as many as he could prudently place on board his schooner ... Robert Sands' kindness to [Susannah Diamond] under such an accumulation of misery was unceasing ...

There was no time, or space, for personal possessions on the *Oracle*. There was barely room for people. Bereaved mother Trijntje de Haan was horrified by what happened as she was helped aboard. Having spent the entirety of the past two days and nights clutching a bag of trinkets, valuables and her dead children's clothing, she was now being forced to relinquish them. Her grandson later said, 'In the confusion of leaving the sinking ship to board the small sloop a sailor snatched away [her] bag. Her weak cries were unheard and she was too near dead to protest. Grandmother never saw her treasures again.'

Captain Robert Sands and his crew made sure Susannah, the other women and their children were securely aboard the *Oracle* and reassured the men that they would be next to leave. 'Amphibian' and the majority of his crew took over the pumps, allowing the exhausted survivors time to rest, as the *Oracle* raced across the sea with all sails set. The little ship was now under the command of Mate William Sands, a brother of the captain and headed for the nearest island that could support such a large number of people. Grand Bahama was approximately 25 miles away, out of sight but very much in mind.

The *Caledonian Mercury* of 3 July 1851 included a letter from a traveller there, describing the area for their readers.

> The Bahamas, as it is well known, comprehend a chain of islands lying to the north of Cuba and St Domingo, which have never been regularly surveyed, or numbered, but have been estimated at about 500. A great proportion of them are little more than cliffs or rocks and the whole of them are for the most part low, flat and rocky ... The people here [in the area of Grand Bahama], indeed nearly throughout the whole of the Bahamas, live principally like lawyers and doctors, on other people's misfortunes. Across the Bahama banks is the grand thoroughfare for all vessels from the United States bound to the southward of the Gulf of Florida ... The navigation is probably the worst in the world, the whole place being full of shoals, banks and rocks. The consequence of this is, that wrecks, particularly during the winter, are so numerous, that many persons, devote their whole time to the occupation of wrecking. It is, however, conducted according to law! The scene of tumult that occurs when there is news of a wreck, reminds one of a nest of hornets rushing out to repel some invasion of their premises.

The *William and Mary* had drifted out of sight of the islands they had previously passed and it was sheer luck that the crew of the *Oracle* had noticed their plight. The *Caledonian Mercury* had also detailed how, 'All vessels that go wrecking are obliged to have a license; and when they have wrecked property on board, are bound to hoist the wrecking flag, which is white, with the number of the license marked in the centre.' And somewhat sniffily admitted that, 'the wreckers do some good occasionally. They save a great many lives, though as they are compelled to do so, they have the less merit ... They are a wild set of lads, though they cannot always be called w–reckless! Excuse the pun if you can.'

Wild or not, Captain Sands and his crew were skilled sailors and deeply sympathetic to the plight of the poor wretches they found aboard the sinking ship. Family men themselves, they sought to calm the fears of the people they were in the process of saving and just their presence was enough to reassure the survivors that all was not lost. It took the crew of the *Oracle* five hours to transport the women and fifty children to Grand Bahama, transfer them safely to the sandy shore, ensure Susannah Diamond was comfortable and return to the *William and Mary*. It must have felt like forever to the men they had left behind, but this was the quickest they could manage.

Wrecking vessels were small, lightweight and built for speed by the local shipyards. Unlike other enterprises in the Bahamas, such as plantation work and the now defunct practice of privateering, wrecking was carried out by Bahamians, supported by Bahamians, for the benefit of Bahamians. It was a key industry for the island chain, dependent on the weather, others' misfortune and a lack of lighthouses – which the Bahamians campaigned against and sabotaged when they could. A few years after Captain Sands and his crew came upon the *William and Mary*, in 1856, almost half of the able-bodied men in the Bahamas were reported to be engaged in the wrecking industry, with 302 vessels licensed as wreckers. The British government considered salvaged goods as imports requiring duty to be paid and made a considerable profit from the Bahamians' activities at sea. Goods salvaged from wrecks counted for more than 50 per cent of the total imports to the Bahamas and, when shipped elsewhere to sell, made up more than two-thirds of the goods exported from these sparsely-populated islands.

Although technically every item salvaged was required to be sent to Nassau for auction, in reality certain items were kept by the wreckers and their families as a perk of the job. Customs officials turned a blind eye to the casks and crates of food, clothing and tackle that made their way into the wreckers' shacks and shanties and ignored the furniture and sailing equipment (like steering wheels, clocks and barometers) that made life that little bit easier at home or on the little ships.

When the *Oracle* approached the *William and Mary* for a second time, there was another wrecker close by, the *Contest*. Together, the vessels took the majority of the remaining survivors on board. There was no room for anything but living cargo, although some of them managed to fill their pockets before leaving. Hendrik Jans Kas, writing home, said, 'Now you will wonder what became of [our] things. Our trunks and all our clothes are partially gone.' His companion, Haagsma, said, 'We were obliged to abandon all of our baggage but that was a matter of minor concern. Our only aim and desire was to save our lives and to that end Providence granted evident aid.'

Sands had hoped to keep pumping water from the hold, aiming, as the emigrants had, to beach the *William and Mary* nearby and salvage the cargo as well as claim his fee for the rescue of the vessel. This was still a possibility, two days after the hull was holed and a day and a half after the captain and majority of the crew abandoned ship and everyone on it. But the majority of the survivors were too exhausted to continue at the pumps, even with the help and encouragement of Captain Sands and his crew and the water inevitably rose around them. Enough was enough and the *Oracle* and its partner departed once again, leaving only a skeleton crew behind to keep pumping.

'[They] took the colony to a sandy shore on a barren island and left them there', wrote Jan Tuininga's grandson. 'And not understanding the language they spoke, the poor people were completely mystified and lost courage. A friend of grandfather's was so cast down that he took an eating fork made from pewter and sticking it into the sand, said, "There, I'll never need that again. All is over and we are left here to die." But grandfather replied, "Not so, I still think there is hope and as an emblem of my faith I'll take this fork" and he picked it up. Grandfather ate with that fork during the rest of his life until there was hardly a tine left on the fork.'

Haagsma recalled his time on the island 'vividly' and with humour.

'Where are we?' that was the first question we asked each other; because at that time we did not know the name of the island. Each person armed himself with something with which to defend himself in case of need. Some of the people rested under the open sky while the others kept watch. And, behold, – soon we were surrounded by enemies. Unashamed they attacked our camp from all sides and, regardless of how we defended ourselves, still several were wounded. But I do not wish to prolong your curiosity any longer; – those enemies were not human ... Mosquitos, a kind of fly, which in a warm climate often attack a traveller, so that the entire head and hands are covered by their somewhat poisonous stings.

Unfortunately, these bloodsucking flies carried viruses, including the often fatal 'yellow jack' or yellow fever. The consequences of the *William and Mary*'s wrecking in the Bahamas were yet to be fully realised by the emigrants currently slapping at the flies bothering them on the beach.

Like Tuininga's friend, Bekius was also initially quite concerned. It seemed as though they had traded one grave for another. He wrote,

[A]gain our prospects appeared black. As it was 7 o'clock in the evening we went to sleep and so passed the night. Then we went into the woods to find some people. But at first we did not succeed. We found only some young oxen, but this assured us that the island was inhabited.

A second time we set out to explore the island. Then we met a man on the shore who approached us in a friendly manner and told us he was the officer of the island, which comforted us. He directed us to a well where we could slake our thirst, next he promised to provide us with food, which he brought but in such small amounts that it refreshed us but did not satisfy our hunger. The reason for the small amount of food was that the inhabitants had to bring all their food from a distance and at this moment had little on hand. Fortunately this lasted only two days. On the second of these days we had nothing to eat. We decided to search for food on the shore in which we were successful; this consisted [of] oysters which we cooked and ate with the greatest relish.

Siebren Wesselius, however, was too tired to care about angry islanders or marauding beasts and appeared somewhat oblivious to his companions' worries. 'We laid ourselves upon the shore and that night had a peaceful sleep.' Haagsma, too, was cheerful. He remembered the day more positively than Bekius.

… a few of us went on a reconnoitring trip and, because of the density of the under-brush, which covered the entire island, follow[ed] the rocks along the shore. Soon we met someone on the other side of the island who approached us peacefully. It was fortunately an agent of the chief officer of the island who apparently had been informed about our situation. He accompanied us to our lodging place and inquired further about what had taken place. Our water and ship's biscuits were soon supplied, which was a treat for us, such as we had never tasted before. Frequently, fishermen came by who furnished some refreshing food.

In the afternoon we made another little trip along the coast and found buildings which are like those in some areas of North Brabant. They were occupied by whites and negroes, all of them being friendly toward us, serving us hospitably with meal-cake, fish and pork and refused to accept anything for it. I was especially amused by a woman who was sitting on a rocking chair, rocking herself with one foot and her child with the other.

Having deposited most of the survivors on the island and notified a settlement nearby of the situation, the crew of the *Oracle* had returned to the wreck to assist Captain Sands and the few survivors who remained there at the pumps. But it was too little, too late. Joseph Brooks, who had chosen to remain at the pumps, recalled later that, 'Captain Sands worked hard to … get the ship to shore … but all to no effect. However, the pumps were kept continually going and we managed to keep her afloat until Friday morning. About 10 o'clock she was fast settling down, the water being level with the second deck. She soon began to sink rapidly and Captain Sands thought it prudent for us all to leave the ship. Some of us got on board his vessel and some were taken up by another vessel called the *Contest* … We had scarce time to get out of the *William and Mary* before down she went and was immediately out of sight.'

They had had a very lucky escape. Haagsma wrote of that Friday, 'On that day our deserted ship really sank. The people who had remained on it to pump, Friesians among them, leaped into one of the lifeboats of the schooner. One of our people had because of confusion not followed the others and sank with the ship into the sea. He surely would have drowned had he not been grabbed immediately when he came up unconscious.' Captain 'Amphibious' Sands was one of the men to swim up through the ship to safety, as the crew watched for sharks and extended strong hands to help the swimmers aboard.

They had escaped with their lives and sacrificed significant financial gain in order to rescue complete strangers. They were heroes. Salvage was a perilous and at times deeply unpleasant experience, but without it many who scraped a living in the beautiful islands of the Bahamas would otherwise starve. Two years prior, the *Caledonian Mercury* of 3 July 1851 contained part of a traveller's letter regarding the general state of living in the Bahamas and the wrecking trade:

> You may suppose they are rather an unquiet race these wreckers; and after the spoil is shared, there is generally a drunken riot ... The other day at March Harbour a wreck occurred. I went up a hill, the usual look-out, to see it. There I found a host of old women snuffling the carcass from afar. I said I thought the vessel was at anchor outside the reef. 'No,' said one of the ancients, 'she's just where she should be,' i.e. on the reef ... The time here occasionally hangs heavy enough. The mosquitoes make sitting still for any length of time almost impossible; and in summer, I am told, they are a thousand times worse than at present, so that some out of door occupation is very desirable.
>
> ... There have been no end of wrecks lately and some of the wreckers have had a fine harvest. One of the vessels cleared 101 dollars for each man. As long as this last[s] they continue on shore and go off to look for more. A few such trips might make them independent, but they are a most improvident race like all who get their living on the deep. In many cases the cargo is recovered by means of divers, so you may suppose their cash is earned hardly enough. Fancy a man diving in 7 fathoms [42 feet] and bringing up a barrel of pork or a box of sugar. This is quite common and the length of time the divers will remain under water is incredible. The other day one of them lost his way in a sunken vessel and forgot to come up again.

Salvage divers also had to deal with other people's mortality face to face and sometimes by touch alone if they dived without lights. The *Staffordshire*

Advertiser of 12 March 1853 included a grim piece on the salvage of the *Queen Victoria*:

> The plate in the Queen Victoria's cabin has been saved by a diver; but the man protests that nothing in the world should induce him to go down a second time, as the scene in the cabin was the most horrible he had ever witnessed. He thought that he had entered a wax work exhibition, the corpses never having moved from their position since the vessel went down. There were some eighteen or twenty persons in the cabin, one and all of whom appeared to be holding conversation with each other; and the general appearance of the whole scene was so lifelike that he was almost inclined to believe that some were yet living.

The divers worked hard and deserved every penny they got.

As the somewhat judgmental letter writer continued in the *Caledonian Mercury* of 3 July 1851,

> [T]he people are too lazy to fish; there is no beef or mutton within these oxless isles; the poultry we keep disappear too fast and vegetables are very scarce. We consequently depend very much on supplies from Nassau, – hams, tinned provisions, &c. As to salt beef and pork, we eschew them and cannot chew them … Should [cholera] come here it will go hard with the Cay. The food of the people, the way in which the houses are huddled together, the filthy habits of the inhabitants, who never wash from fear of catching cold and the want of all medical assistance, will possibly be the means of solving a medical problem [i.e. through death].

The survivors now stranded on the island of Grand Bahama were lucky to have received any food at all from the inhabitants there. Their lot could have been far worse, as detailed in the *Northern Star and Leeds General Advertiser* of 1 May 1852. A Captain Gardiner, described as 'a gentleman of fortune', had vanished near the Falkland Islands having joined the Patagonian Missionary Society and 'gone to some small barren islands off the Horn to enlighten the inhabitants, wild as they were' and HMS *Dido* was instructed to search for him. They were horrified by what they found.

> I beheld a sight, the which I trust I shall never witness again. Strewed in different parts of the beach were Capt. G. and two of his party. The first we saw was Capt. G. in a state of decomposition. We supposed it to be him, by there being a watch hanging to his skeleton form; and some distance from him there was another. We proceeded some distance to a cave with a lantern; when we entered there was a deadly smell at the end of the cave, where we found the remains of the others. There were furniture and cooking utensils, as though they had lived there some time. The boats' crews were allowed to have the clothes, &c., as they found a large chest, containing books and clothing and on the lid of it was nailed his will, stating that the first ship that found them should have them. We buried them with the honours of war. And cut on the wall was this inscription – 'Proceed on the beach about a mile-and-a-half; you will find three more; do not delay, for we are starving.' We made the best of haste and found them dead. It appeared they had been shunned by the natives and had starved to death.

Considering how little the islanders had and how much they shared with the survivors of the *William and Mary*, their generosity towards this huge group of complete strangers is striking and commendable. After another night of camping on the shore, listening to the rustle of nocturnal creatures through the undergrowth nearby and the rush and retreat of waves on the sand as the tide came and went, they had a visitor. Some of the survivors were called for by locals and taken to the city of Nassau, on New Providence Island, so they could report what happened to the consuls there. Among them were some of the more visibly unwell emigrants. It is likely that Susannah Diamond was taken for medical treatment in the barracks there at the same time. She was now ill with the dreaded yellow fever. The poor woman, having lost her tiny baby on the ship and her husband to the longboat, was crying out for him, desperate with worry and fearful that he had been drowned in the Atlantic. There was little anyone could do to reassure her.

According to Haagsma, the rest of the survivors 'remained on the island that day and refreshed themselves with oysters and clear spring-water. The next night we were taken on two vessels … Provisions were bought from time to time, although there is not much to be had anywhere …' They ate bacon, buckwheat, fish and turtle-soup while they sailed. The boats called into settlements on the way to New Providence and Haagsma and the others were fascinated by the way of life there. 'All of the Bahama [I]slands are under British rule. There are no slaves; the negro is just as free and independent as the white resident.'

Occasionally the survivors were allowed to venture ashore, too. Haagsma noted that 'a white inhabitant, among other things told me that there 215 people had been shipwrecked in two months, all of whom were taken to New Orleans by way of Nassau. From that ship the captain was not the first but the last to leave the ship.'

When they sighted Nassau one evening, they were entranced. This was the largest settlement in the Bahamas, which had been a British Crown Colony since 1718. Haagsma in particular was impressed with what they saw. 'The view of the newly-built city was beautiful, undoubtedly enhanced by the sparkling evening sun; – for us who had been separated from social life for fifty days.' As they came closer, the fear, deprivation and excitement of the previous week proved too much for 29-year-old Frisian Petrus van der Tol. Having survived the journey, the wreck and the rescue, it seems particularly cruel that he died within sight of Nassau. He was not the last of the party to die in the Bahamas.

The next morning the remaining survivors were put ashore and 'conducted to a well-organised building where we were refreshed with food and drink. Then we were glad we had not leaped into the [long]boat, because our situation was certainly more favourable than that of the three Friesians. Besides, we had a few extra clothes, while I had seen one of those who left dressed in trousers held up by a rope, without a coat or a vest, with one and a half of a wooden-shoe [probably Izaak Roorda] and without provisions for such an uncertain trip.'

The people of the Bahamas, no matter their own circumstances and difficulties, pulled together and donated time, food, money and clothing to the survivors flooding the island. The *Bahama Herald* of 14 May 1853 printed an appeal to the islanders for help:

> The attention of the Christian Public of New Providence is earnestly solicited to the dreadful calamity which has befallen the [*William and Mary*] in the almost total loss of the property of [173] passengers, the majority of whom are of the poorer classes ... [T]he lives of these emigrants have been providentially saved, but the majority of them have been brought to Nassau so destitute of clothing, as to furnish a strong ground of appeal to the compassion of the community ... [I]t is confidently expected that the Christian charity which on former occasions were so cheerfully extended to our suffering fellow creatures will not on the present be less cheerfully or liberally bestowed.

This appeal was a great success and four days later the *Nassau Guardian* proudly reported,

> THE WRECKED EMIGRANTS. – We have much pleasure in recording the benevolent acts of a committee of ladies of our town, who have been administering to the necessities of the unfortunate emigrants wrecked in the Am. ship '*William and Mary*' by superintending the making up of articles of clothing for the most destitute at the Public Buildings. Collections will also be made in their behalf at the various places of worship on Sunday next.

Jan Tuininga's grandson describes him saying that, 'they were tenderly cared for and nursed back to health' and the hard-to-please Bekius later wrote that, 'we were brought to a house set aside for shipwrecked people. Half starved we arrived but now food was again given to us in ample amounts.... Wherever we moved along the streets, they offered us bread and many gave us money. But in this respect I shall not praise our people; our Christians should use this as a mirror in which to compare their own acts.'

The deeply religious Haagsma added to this, saying,

The inhabitants belong to the white and negro races, or rather copper-colored and make a good living. They showed a very generous attitude toward us and provided for needs with money they had collected. Everyone there seems to take pride in doing something for others and their deeds have the mark of a Christian religion which they profess ... [O]n Pent[e]cost we were enable[d], with the congregation to offer our silent prayers to Him who had so remarkable saved us when our souls were oppressed by the fear of death.

Next to die was 45-year-old carpenter's mate Jacob Sakes Kooistra. Travelling with his wife and children, he had suffered the loss of his youngest son and daughter a month prior as the *William and Mary* crossed the Atlantic. His body was buried in Nassau and his widow Antje left to carry on the journey to America with their three sons, 12-year-old Sake, Tiete, 11, and four-year-old Sijmon.

Meanwhile, in the Western Barracks, Susannah's health was deteriorating. John Gregory, the Governor of the islands, wrote, '[I] sent for a medical man and all that human science can suggest has since been done for her. The poor creature was nearly half immersed in water when she gave birth to the child. My wonder is that she survived the eight days to reach Nassau. Her sufferings are greatly aggravated by her fears about her husband but from all I can learn I think he will cast up hereafter as a few of the emigrants <u>were</u> allowed to get into the ships boats and he may have been one of them.' Local healthcare workers, Dr Chipman and Mrs Capern, had taken over from Dr van der Veer and the unnamed Frisian midwife. They cared for her as she lay dying, still desperate with worry for her husband.

The symptoms of yellow fever, so-called because of the lemon-yellow colour of its jaundiced victims, are deeply unpleasant. It is also sometimes known as 'black vomit' because of the internal bleeding it can induce and the consequent regurgitation of blood. As well as bleeding from both ends, other symptoms included headaches, severe muscular pains, bruising, nausea and constipation. There is no cure and treatments were limited to rest, drinking plenty of fluids and the application of dubiously helpful salves and tonics.

Physicians reported two different kinds of haemorrhage in patients suffering from yellow fever, one occurring when the 'interior walls of ...

some of the larger veins were gone, giving the surface something of the appearance of the tracks which earthworms make in moist ground'. The other occurred in the mucous membranes and upper digestive tract and resulted in the patient vomiting blood with very little effort that looked like coffee grounds and was 'thrown considerable distance'. Susannah's organs eventually failed and she died aged 19 on the morning of Monday 23 May in the Baptist Mission House to the sorrow of many.

As her family grieved and the garrison's British commander, Major d'Arcy, bought a marker for the grave she now occupied in St Matthew's burial ground, the rest of the emigrants were exploring the town. There was little else for them to do as they awaited orders to board the vessels that had answered the advert the Governor had placed in the local newspapers, like this one in the *Bahama Herald* of 14 May 1853:

WANTED

Transport for New Orleans ...
Hire of a Vessel or Vessels
to convey about 150 shipwrecked Emigrants, their stores, etc., from Nassau to New Orleans.... A sample of good wholesome water, fuel for cooking, proper cooking apparatus and the necessary fittings, must be provided by the party whose tender may be accepted.

It was the emigrants' bad luck, as Governor Gregory noted in a despatch to England, that they were experiencing such a delay in Nassau, as,

We are particularly unfortunate in having no vessel in harbour fit to convey so large a party of emigrants to New Orleans. A month ago in the case of the *Osborne* [also shipwrecked] we were more fortunate. The emigrants in that case were all forwarded in a large vessel the *Polar Star* and I have heard of their safe arrival at New Orleans. But situated as we now are I had no alternative but to take up two small vessels the *Time* and the *Rover* at a cost of £540 and I hope to see the greater part of the emigrants off in the course of the next week. Mr Pinder is actively engaged as Emigration Officer in superintending the fitting up of the vessels in accordance (as far as circumstances will admit) with the requirements of the Passengers Act 1852. I fear that they cannot make room for all and after they are gone [I] must do the best I can to send on the few who will be left behind.

Haagsma was making the best of his enforced stay in the Bahamas and his enthusiasm for immigrating west to America was undimmed by the difficulties he and his companions had already faced.

[T]here was the fort called 'Charlotte' which had been completely hewn from a rock with a number of underground passages and rooms and certainly may be called a masterpiece of fortress architecture. I was shown, among other things, the underground room in which the governor hid when the fort was surrendered to the English … Among the interesting things to see in the city [of Nassau] is the statue of Columbus. On the base is inscribed 'Columbus' and just below it '1492' the year in which that great man discovered America and as a result opened a rich source of prosperity for the inhabitants of the old world.

But whether America would prove prosperous for the 172 would-be immigrants was still to be seen.

Chapter Eleven

As you are aware, probably, those on board and who were lost, were all emigrants, seeking an asylum in free and happy America; and because they were emigrants, the case, awful as it is excites very little notice or remark and why is this? Were not those who were lost flesh and blood as we are? Had they not ties that bound them as closely to this world as any which we possess? Were there not fathers and mothers in that immense crowd who were engulfed in death's waters and who have left behind them sons and daughters who will weep bitterly at their loss? Of this there can surely be no doubt and yet these 175 souls suddenly perish without exciting more than a momentary remark. The intelligence of the disaster reached us yesterday – today it is forgotten! Had the accident happened nearer our own doors and there had been among the lost twenty or even a dozen our everyday companions, the case would have been different – it would have touched the chord of public feeling and sympathy and afforded a subject of serious thought for a few days at least.

(*New Orleans Picayune*, 25 May 1853)

After the Rescue, May 1853 onwards

While the women of the Bahamas procured material, buttons and thread and made articles of clothing for the survivors currently stranded on the island, suitable vessels were sought to ferry the less unwell past Florida to the port of New Orleans. Eventually the schooners *Time*, *Rover* and *Clyde* were hired for the purpose and outfitted appropriately with plentiful food and water.

Sjoerd Bekius was delighted to be on his way and no longer travelling with the other parties, who he had harsh words for despite his own happiness. 'June 1 was the day of our departure and after having had the doctor on board, we set out to sea with a strong northeast wind. It was then a great deal more peaceful on the ship than usual; since the Irish left on another schooner. Some twenty Irish and German, who were to be picked up later, remained.' As they had on the *William and Mary*, the emigrants naturally separated into groups according to nationality or shared language. The Frisians sailed for New Orleans in early June aboard the *Time*, while the majority of the English, Irish and Scots travelled on the *Rover* shortly after. Some of the survivors lingered in the Bahamas, recovering from illnesses and injuries in their boarding houses and eventually taking passage in the *Clyde*.

Peter McDonald, the disgraced cook who had suffered so at the hands of the crew for stealing food from the captain to give to the passengers, does not show up in the records for any of the schooners leaving the Bahamas at the time. He may have decided to stay put or perhaps have travelled under a false name to New Orleans. Fifty-year-old James Burke shows up on the manifests for both the *Rover* and the *Clyde*. It is highly unlikely that there were two men of the same name and age on the *William and Mary* at the same time. But quite what this subterfuge achieved is impossible to know now.

Bonnema's party, their names unfamiliar to the men writing out the passenger lists and therefore almost unrecognisable in their spellings, carried on their journey. Bekius wrote how on 8 June, 'we sailed into the Mississippi River. Its mouth is almost 400 feet wide there and covered with reeds or other green growth ... We stared about at the beautiful river banks, which were there decked in a luxurious green and lovely woods, presenting a beautiful scene. Now and then we would collide with a large tree-trunk many of which float down the river, when the women would moan, again, thinking that the rocks of the Bahama Bank were also found in the Mississippi.'

It was a nerve-wracking experience for them to continue travelling by water, but unless they chose to settle in the Bahamas – which would have been utterly impracticable – they had no choice but to go on. What they heard next enraged them. As Bekius recalled, 'I heard from the captain that the small boat with the crew of the William and Mary had been rescued and that the people were in an American port. The captain had made a report regarding the shipwreck and the following appeared in the newspaper: "the ship William and Mary went aground near the Bahama Islands. A total of 200 passengers died in the waves. Only the captain and a few members of the crew saved themselves in life-boats. The ship sank so fast that the captain had difficulty in leaving it." As soon as we heard that our captain sent a telegram to New Orleans reporting that the so-called lost passengers were coming up the river.'

This would put the cat well and truly among the pigeons as far as Captain Stinson and his crew were concerned. But Bekius was not to know of the impact the reports of their continued survival would have for some time yet. He was optimistic about his future and continued, '[W]e again came into picturesque areas, interspersed with sugar plantations and beautiful woods, while here and there new villages arose or were being enlarged. There was evidence everywhere of wealth and prosperity. I have as yet not seen poverty in America. If one has ambition he need have no fear of want, because a laborer or tradesman earns twice as much here as he does in Friesland and can live just as cheaply.'

The British and Irish emigrants had similar hopes, dreams and aspirations of success to the Frisians, but a different way of working towards achieving them. Instead of travelling en masse and building a new community together, these disparate individuals, who had gotten to know each other well during their hellish journey, dispersed on reaching New Orleans, meeting friends and family, taking up positions or continuing on their journey.

The Irish emigrants, so often unwelcome in Scotland and England, now travelled within a country that, according to the *Freeman's Journal* of 8 April 1852, embraced their presence, energy and talents, although in reality there was also a lot of anti-Irish and sometimes anti-Catholic feeling around too. There was, as usual, no mention of the tribes already living there, nor any acknowledgment of non-white races.

The greater the number of emigrants ... who visit our shores, the greater and the more vast will be our prosperity and the more rapidly will the wealth and power of the nation be unfolded ... They people our savannahs and prairies, clear our forests, cultivate the teeming soil, build our railroads and cities and introduce the mechanical arts in which Europeans excel and in a few years Europe is repaid by improvements on what she gave. Emigration not only increases the population but improves the race on this continent, for it is always the most vigorous, healthy and energetic who emigrate; and this, with the crossing of breeds, is one great cause of the go-a-head character of the American people.

It would likely have been a good place for Irishman John Diamond to settle and raise a family, but that simply was not to be, given his escape in the longboat. Instead, his late wife Susannah's grieving parents and sisters, the Stewarts, carried on their journey to mining districts inland. Bridget Donnelly, 23, was joining her husband in Indiana. The Burns family were returning to Philadelphia and Joseph Brooks and his wife, Mary Ann, were leaving for Navasota, Texas. A few took the time to swear to affidavits detailing their exploits on the *William and Mary* before carrying on their journey, but it was not a healthy place to stay for long as a visitor, especially at that time of year.

According to the *Wells Journal* of 21 February 1852,

On reaching New Orleans, the steerage-passengers endure great exposure on the open decks of the steam-boat for many successive days and nights. Tempted, too, by the tropical fruits and vegetables, so grateful after a long voyage, but which rapidly decay, especially in hot weather, thousands who have escaped the yellow-fever of New Orleans perish by cholera – a St. Louis paper, before us, stating that half of one steamer's list had been buried there by that fearful scourge within ten days after landing and attributing the mortality to the causes just glanced at.

It was now early June and summer in New Orleans was a far cry from summer in Western Europe. The area was prone to rainfall, even while at its warmest, and the warm moist atmosphere lent itself to disease and deeply unpleasant deaths from cholera, dysentery and yellow fever among others. A long and grisly account in the *Royal Cornwall Gazette* of 9 September 1853 warned families and friends of the survivors what to expect if they were contemplating making the journey across the Atlantic to join them.

The annals of Pestilence can scarcely match the horrors which are now occurring at New Orleans. Situated among the swamps towards the mouth of the Mississippi, with an intense summer climate and nothing to mitigate the violence of the heat and the depressing influence of reeking malaria, it is pre-eminently a hotbed of disease under ordinary circumstances … We knew before that New Orleans was a city where men braved disease and death to get money; where the most reckless would naturally congregate and where knavery, violence and slave-driving, the gaming table, the pistol and the bowie knife prevailed, beyond every other town in the Union, probably beyond every other place on earth … The following description of a visit to the cemeteries is from a New Orleans paper – there are columns of such horrors:

At the gathering points carriages accumulated and vulgar teamsters, as they jostled each other in the press, mingled the coarse jest with the ribald oath; no sound but of profane malediction and of riotous mirth, the clang of whipthongs and the rattle of wheels. At the gates the winds brought intimation of the corruption working within. Not a puff but was laden with the rank atmosphere from rotting corpses. Inside they were piled by fifties, exposed to the heat of the sun, swollen with corruption, bursting their coffin lids, sundering, as if by physical effort, the ligaments that bound their hands and feet and extending their rigid limbs in every outré attitude. What a feast of horrors! Inside, corpses piled in pyramids and without the gates old and withered crones and fat huxter-women, fretting in their own grease, dispensing ice creams and confections and brushing away with brooms made of bushes, the green bottleflies that hovered on their merchandise and which anon buzzed away to drink dainty inhalations from the green and festering corpses.

… Long ditches were dug across the human charnel. Wide enough were they to entomb a legion, but only 14 inches deep. Coffins laid in them showed their tops above the surface of the earth. On these was piled dirt to the depth of a foot or more, but so loosely, that myriads of flies found entry between the loose clods, down to the cracked seams of the coffins and buzzed and blew their ova, creating each hour their new hatched swarms.

… Now and then the mattock or the spade would disturb the bones of some former tenant of the mould, forgotten there amid the armies of the accumulated victims and the sturdy labourer with a gyre would hurl the broken fragments on the sward, growl forth an energetic d——n and chuckle in his excess of glee. Skull bones were dug up from their long sepulture [*sic* – sepulchre], with ghastliness staring out 'From each lacklustre, eyeless hole,' without eliciting an 'Alas, poor Yorick,' and with only an exclamation from the digger of 'Room for your betters.'

Economy of space was the source of the cunning calculation in stowing away the dead men. Side by side were laid two, of gigantic proportions, bloated by corruption to the size of Titans. The central projections of their coffins left spaces between them at their heads and heels. This was too much room to be filled with earth. How should the space be saved? Opportunely the material is at hand, for a cart comes lumbering in, with the corpses of a mother and her two little children. Chuck the children into the space at the heads and heels of the Titans and lay the mother by herself out there alone. A comrade for her will be found anon and herself and babes will sleep not the less soundly from the unwonted contact.

There was a grim practicality at work, which the Frisian party managed to avoid, as did many if not all of their fellow sufferers from the shipwreck. Their luck appeared to have changed, though unfortunately not for long, and Bekius delighted in his first sight of New Orleans. 'When the morning of June 10 dawned that capital of the business of the southern states lay before us. In the golden rays of the morning sun the scene was beautiful. Those colossal, mostly white buildings, those hundreds of gigantic steamboats and those luxurious banks on each side of the winding river, presented an [u]nsurpassable scene.'

They soon changed vessels for another, one that would transport them upriver to St Louis. There was time for the immigrants to stretch their legs and explore a little before returning to the stink of the steamer, which the author Harriet Beecher Stowe described as 'not at all fragrant; in short, particularly in a steamer, there is a most mournful combination of grease, steam, onions and dinners in general, either past, present, or to come, which, floating invisibly in the atmosphere, strongly predisposes to that disgust of existence which, in half-an-hour after sailing, begins to come upon you', (*Belfast News-Letter*, 16 August 1854). Beecher Stowe, who had written the nineteenth century's most popular novel, *Uncle Tom's Cabin*, not far from where the *William and Mary* was built in Maine and was appearing at Anti-Slavery meetings in Scotland while the ship made its return journey across the Atlantic, had found her steamer journey on the Mississippi deeply and unexpectedly unpleasant. But for the Frisians who had already experienced the trauma of a wreck and the treachery of abandonment, it seemed generally all right.

Bekius was happily people-watching and later wrote,

[E]veryone was preparing to go aboard. It is an interesting sight to see such a busy moment. The free American, the staid Englishman, the congenial German, the vivacious Frenchman and the lumbering Spaniard there loose [*sic*] all their characteristics and look for a place on the boats. Here one will see a group of immigrants arriving and there an American hunter with a ham on his shoulder with a fine dog walking at his side, who has his eye on the ham rather than on its master. New Orleans has real clean streets and beautiful buildings … However, where the city is not as built-up, there are also streets which seem to call to the traveller, 'come and help us!'

Meanwhile, across the Atlantic, the survivors rescued from the leaky longboat by the *Pollux* were regaining their land-legs in Liverpool after so many weeks at sea and telling their own version of events to journalists, officials and people on the street. Suddenly Stinson's version of events, questionable at the best of times, was coming completely apart.

The *New York Times* of 18 May 1853 was already deeply and publicly suspicious of the captain's conduct and hinting at dark deeds and deception.

The narrative of the loss of the bark *William and Mary*, off the Bahama Islands, has been but imperfectly set before the public. The silence of the Captain of the vessel is not a little remarkable. His sudden disappearance from the City is not less so. There must be reasons for this conduct and what they are the community would be glad to know. In these days of catastrophes, when one tale of wo[e] treads so closely upon another, that room is scarcely left for thought, the least that can be expected, is a careful and authentic statement of the causes and extent of each new disaster. Nothing of this character has been attempted in the present instance. The calamity is suddenly announced and is soon ended, so far as Captain STINSON is concerned. Some considerations naturally suggest themselves in connection with the subject.

... The reef on which the bark struck is well-known to all navigators. It is laid down with care upon all approved charts and there seems to be very little excuse for any man in his senses running upon it. It is claimed, in extenuation, that the weather had become hazy, that navigation was difficult and the Captain supposed he was on the right track. The palliation is scarcely satisfactory. To say that a reef cannot be seen, is no reason for running a ship in a direction where it is known to lie. Another point in this business is unpleasantly conspicuous. It is evident that very few and exceedingly futile efforts were made for the rescue of the passengers after the destruction of the vessel appeared inevitable. The captain was by no means so prompt in command as the exigency of the case demanded.

They, and other newspapers, put pressure on Stinson and eight days later prompted him again for answers he was unwilling or unable to give.

It was obviously the duty of the Captain to keep in shoal water and if possible to get further on the Bank. But if this could not be done, the spars should have been cut away and rafts formed sufficiently large, in addition to the boats, to contain all the passengers and crew. In this way it is probable that the lives of all, or nearly all, on board, could have been saved, especially as hardly a day passes in which a merchant ship or a 'wrecker' does not pass over that part of the Great Bahama Bank. The statement made by Captain STINSON, thus far, is vague and unsatisfactory. The public look to him to account for the loss of nearly two hundred lives and they have a right to know how far he is responsible for this fearful calamity.

They and the grieving families and friends of the emigrants and sailors declared dead after the vessel supposedly sank before Stinson's eyes, were delighted to hear that on the contrary, all but a few were still very much alive. On 31 May 1853 the *New York Times* reported the glad tidings and said, 'It is like life from the dead'. The *Spirit of the Times* effused on 7 June 1853 that, 'No news item of the month has been so worthy of rejoicing over, as the intelligence of the rescue and safety of the emigrant passengers of the ship William and Mary, wrecked amongst the Bahamas on its way from Liverpool to New Orleans. About one hundred and seventy human beings, given up to the waves and monsters of the deep, rescued by wreckers, it seems, while their sinking coffin was tumbling about among rocks and breakers and just ready to make the fatal plunge, are thus happily saved.'

It would take a while for the news to cross the Atlantic and spread across Ireland, Britain, Germany and Friesland. However, the newspapers there were alert to the possibility of news of wreckage, salvage, or survivors plucked from the water. The *Freeman's Journal* kept the story alive on their pages despite a total lack of further information, saying on 8 June 1853, 'There is nothing further, regarding the loss of the William and Mary, on which occasion nearly 200 lives were lost. The captain and owners seemed to take it very coolly.'

One of the Commissioners of Emigration for the State of New York, Friedrich Kapp, explained in 1870 that to those engaged in the shipping industry, emigrants were not even worth the same as a box of goods and were 'handled with less care, as they did not break, nor, if injured, require to be paid for'. They were also able to load themselves on and off a vessel, saving further costs and acted as a form of ballast – albeit a moving one – in an otherwise near-empty ship.

It was actually in the shipowners interests, financially at least, to lose the passengers along with the ship if the vessel was British-owned or, as was the case with the American *William and Mary*, sailing with British passengers from a British port. As the *Dublin Evening Mail* explained on 6 October 1852, there was compensation to be paid to survivors under the 'new emigration act … In case of any disaster at sea the passengers are (as far as is possible), to be provided with a passage in another ship and to be maintained in the meantime. Governors and consuls may send on shipwrecked passengers and charge the owners of the ship with a crown debt.'

The *Savannah Republican* spelled it out for their readers on 31 May 1853, '[T]he British Passenger Act of 1852, makes full provisions for disasters of this kind and the entire cost of maintaining these passengers, although borne, in the first instance, by the British Government, becomes, by a section of that act, a Crown debt and is recoverable from the 'owner, master, agents and charterers' of the ship – a bond being given at the port from whence the ship sails to cover any such contingencies. The cost of maintaining the passengers at Nassau and transporting them to New-Orleans, will be about $1,000.'

Sjoerd Bekius of the Frisian party elaborated on this further, 'The expense of our stay was charged to the account of the owner[s] of the lost ship and that amounted to quite a total, when you figure: 1 pound of bread, 1 pound of beef or pork, 3 ounces of rice, 1 ounce of sugar and ½ ounce of coffee per person, per day for 200 people. Besides the inhabitants distributed to each individual: 1 white jacket and trousers, 1 shirt, 1 hat and 1 pair of shoes and in addition to all of that we received 1 dollar apiece when we left.'

If everyone that Stinson and his crew had abandoned on the sinking ship had died, it would have saved the owners – including Stinson's father-in-law – a lot of money, as well as the shame of being associated with such an enormous embarrassment. And Stinson was nowhere to be seen.

The *New York Times* of 4 June 1853 called Stinson 'The Runaway Captain.' They went on to say,

The circumstances of this case are not a little peculiar. The fault, as in too many cases, is traceable to the manifest incompetency of the officers of the ship. The event has proved that there was not only a possibility of preserving the vessel, but the lives of all the persons on board of her. In three or four hours' time, according to the accounts we now receive, the bark could have been run ashore and her cargo could have been saved. The Captain and his mates evinced altogether too much anxiety to be gone from an unpleasant scene. The small boats were swung off in marvellous haste and the few who succeeded in manning them pushed away in eager speed, leaving the despairing wretches on board to shift for themselves as they might.

The statements of the rescued parties indicate very clearly that the direction and energetic control, by the Captain and his officers, of the motley crew of emigrants on board, would have precluded all danger of ultimate disaster. A hundred measures to insure the safety of the ship could then have been adopted, which were totally unknown to the unskilled men left to die. A wrecking schooner, the last place from which aid might naturally be expected in such an emergency, finally succeeded in rescuing all but two of the passengers and crew remaining on board the ship and the destitute emigrants are now lodged and fed, poorly enough, at the small port of Nassau, in the Bahamas.

The course pursued by Captain STINSON in forsaking his vessel and afterward reporting his meagre statement that the ship went down, probably with all on board, is such as to awaken lively sentiments of indignation. The narrative of the rescue indicates that great fault lies at a single door and there can be no apology for a neglect of duty so palpable and so cruel.

Stinson didn't even bother to try.

He may have thought something along the lines of 'least said, soonest mended', or been advised to try and let it blow over. Perhaps he hoped for another, juicier scandal to divert attention from his craven deeds and take up precious inches in the press. Whatever was going through his mind, the hard-bitten journalists of Britain and America were having none of it.

A month after Stinson and the crewmen he'd allowed in the lifeboat had arrived in New York on the *Reuben Carver*, the newspapers were still full of condemnation for them. The *Lewisburg Chronicle* of 17 June 1853 wrote, 'the captain and crew at the beginning of danger seized upon the boats and deserted the vessel, leaving the passengers in utter helplessness and despair. Such inhumanity is almost incredible and merits the execrations of the world.' And on the other side of the Atlantic, the *Leeds Times* of 18 June 1853 stated,

It now seems that the craven wretches who commanded and navigated that vessel, at the first suggestion of danger, instead of exerting themselves to save the helpless passengers in their charge, seized upon the only means of escape, the ship's boats and rushed for the land, which they reached in safety. As the story was told by these men on their arrival in this city, it was bad enough and sufficient to call down severe censure upon their heads. But this story was that they only left the ship at the moment of her sinking and when further effort was totally unavailing. The truth now seems to be that the desertion of the ship and passengers was at the beginning of the difficulty and when everything was to be done to prevent the water from gaining in the hold, to make signals for succour and to manage the ship so as to aid in the final safety of the passengers. But the whole 208 souls were mercilessly left to their fate and their despair and helplessness rendered perfect, by the desertion of those who alone seemed competent to save the freight of living beings and whose leaving was taken to be the certain evidence that the doom of those left behind was inevitable. We know of no excuse or palliation for conduct like this. No language can be used to characterise men so destitute of every manly and generous quality, as the officers and crew of the *William and Mary* have shown themselves to be, which could be deemed unjustifiably harsh or improperly severe. They are cowards without souls and should be stamped with the reprobation of all men.

The *New York Times* quoted the *Bahama Herald* on 24 June 1853, continuing to needle those culpable, seeking some kind of reaction or resolution. 'The statement that there was "ten feet of water in the hold," is denied by the three seamen who abode in the ship and the most intelligent of the passengers. She had but five feet and this was reduced by the passengers after the base and cowardly desertion of the captain, mates and crew, to two feet; and had there been hands enough on board to work the ship, she might with all ease and certainty have been run ashore.'

Almost two months after the *William and Mary* was wrecked, the *New Orleans Daily Crescent* was still presenting a case against Stinson and some of the crew, repeating the *Bahama Herald*'s assertions and saying on 30 June 1853,

From the affidavits taken here and verbal statements of the passengers, it appears that the Captain and the crew were chiefly engaged, after the ship struck on Tuesday night, in preparing the boats and making preparations to abandon the ship and passengers to their fate … The ship and cargo might have been saved, as it was, after the Captain's desertion, if the chain had not been slipped, as the wreckers sight the place every twenty-four hours and Capt. Sands stated he could have saved her after he got on board, if the passengers would have continued at the pumps; but in the excitement, uncertainty and eagerness to save their lives (which was all natural and proper) they forsook the pumps altogether.

It was now abundantly clear to the public, the governments, the insurance brokers and marine officials on both sides of the Atlantic that there was something deeply amiss here. People called for official inquiries, some kind of investigation into what had happened and why and how to prevent it from happening again. No-one seemed to ask who stood to gain from such a terrible accident, or whether it may have been deliberate. Despite there being several different accounts of emigrants murdered with a hatchet during the abandonment of the *William and Mary*, or at the very least injured by a crewman and left to die in shark-infested water, there was no official move – at least, not in public – to prosecute or even properly investigate the matter. There were rumours amongst the survivors of their situation being the result of an attempted insurance scam, but with other calamities to report and probably considerable pressure from the maritime authorities and shipping companies to bury the story, the coverage diminished and eventually ceased. Whether the insurers paid out or not is now unknown.

Three years earlier, the Agent for Government and General Emigration at the busy port of Plymouth on the south coast of England, a Mr. J. B. Wilcocks, had told the *Royal Cornwall Gazette* of 19 April 1850

It should never be forgotten, that ill-treatment is the exception and not the rule and that where irregularities have occurred in one ship, a hundred have accomplished their voyages under prosperous and happy circumstances ... because culpable conduct has existed in one or two ships, a whole fleet is condemned and hundreds of men of high honour and integrity in the situation of shipowners, charterers, brokers, captains, mates, surgeons, &c. &c., are mercilessly and undeservedly visited with opprobrium. It must be remembered that life on board ship is necessarily different from that to which the passengers have previously been accustomed; and when, as it sometimes happens, one or two restless or quarrelsome persons form part of the company, the voyage is to a certain extent rendered uncomfortable.

He was right, but terrible tales of death and dishonour at sea and families left to drown or be eaten by sharks by cowardly captains understandably served to discourage would-be emigrants from leaving the comparative safety of land, or from following a particular route or using a particular line's vessels if they did so.

Some were using the coverage of the *William and Mary* to their advantage, suggesting that if the passengers had taken along patented mattresses that doubled as life preservers things would have been easier. Underwriters in the Bahamas were also taking the opportunity to press for more lighthouses there, despite opposition from wrecking communities who would struggle yet more without salvage operations to pick a living from.

The *Morning Courier and Enquirer* of 5 June 1853 said, 'now that the death shriek of a hecatomb of victims swells the appeal, it is to be hoped that procrastination will no longer be indulged in [regarding] the necessity for the erection of a light-house near the rock known as the "Isaacs," upon which the late dreadful shipwreck occurred'. The government went on to submit a proposal for erecting and maintaining the lighthouse, the fourth in the Bahamas, to Parliament. The newspaper also poured yet more vitriol on the captain and his crew, saying, 'If this is human nature, humanity has sunk low indeed. Deeds such as these are fit to make every true man hide his face for shame.'

Something else was being lobbied for in addition to the lighthouse and it provided a stark contrast to Stinson's cowardly actions. Captain Robert Sands' extreme bravery and valour and complete selflessness when saving strangers from the wreck – almost losing his own life in the process – had not gone unnoticed. The Governor of the Bahamas, John Gregory, among other people, pressed for the wrecker and his crew to have some kind of official token of esteem as well as some form of financial recompense to make up for the loss of the goods they ignored in favour of saving people. He wrote to the British Government,

The frightful occurrence of shipwrecks on our widely dispersed islands more particularly where emigrants are on board suggests to me that if Your Grace would be kind enough to give directions either through the Admiralty or the Ordinance that some small token of the Queen's Approbation (ex.g. a plain but useful [teles]cope with a suitable inscription on it) should be presented to the man who first bore down to the sinking ship and exhibited such active humanity in saving the unhappy emigrants the pride as well as the humane feelings of the wrecking population of these islands would receive a most powerful stimulus.

I might indeed do it myself, but I know full well that the smallest token of approbation which emanates from the Sovereign of these Realms would acquire a value far higher than the most costly present from the Governor of the Colony. Robert Sands as the Master of the *Oracle* wrecking schooner is of course the individual, to whom I should recommend this token to be presented but I should moreover be glad to be enabled to make some small present to those of the crew of the *Oracle* who with Sands risked their own lives by staying on board the sinking ship with the remainder of the passengers who could not be carried off in the first trip of the *Oracle* to Grand Bahama. Perhaps it would also be right to reward the Master of the *Contest* the second wrecking vessel that came to the relief.

Captain Sands received a far greater tribute than an engraved telescope. A letter to Governor Gregory from Downing Street, London, written on 30 July 1853, said,

Sir,

At the request of the Royal National Institution for the Preservation of Lives from Shipwreck, I transmit the accompanying communication addressed to Major [...] in the Bahamas. It contains the Silver Medal of the Institution voted by the Committee of Management to Mr. Robert Sands, Master of the Wrecking Schooner '*Oracle*,' in approbation of his exertions in saving from drowning the passengers of the ship '*William and Mary*,' bound from Liverpool to New Orleans, the particulars of whose wreck are repeated in your Despatch No. 46, of the 28th of May.

In addition to the Medal thus awarded, you will be pleased to express to Mr. Robert Sands and his crew, (namely, Benjamin Roberts, James Roberts, Octavius Dorsett, John Cash and Richard Sands) the sense which Her Majesty entertains of the service they have rendered on this occasion, service not limited to the saving of life in the particular instance, but enhanced by the example of generosity and courage shown by the numerous body of their fellow Colonists engaged in an occupation so trying to the character as that of wrecking.

This letter was reproduced in the newspapers throughout the islands and the *Bahama Herald* of 14 September 1853 said, 'If we may be bold enough to venture a hint, we should say that a presentation in public, on some day to be fixed, would be not only gratifying to Mr. Sands and his friends, but to the entire class of persons following the same calling as himself and be incentive to all engaged in so perilous an employment as wrecking.' The pressure was on.

Sadly, Governor John Gregory died of fever before he could present Captain Sands with the medal he so richly deserved. However, Lt. Governor C. R. Nesbitt was happy to proceed. His address to Captain Sands at the ceremony in the Government House in Nassau was included in the *Nassau Guardian* of 2 November 1853,

Captain Sands,

I have much pleasure in seeing you for the purpose of presenting to you, in the presence of Major d'Arcy, Commanding the Troops and other gentlemen here assembled, the Silver Medal of the Royal National Institution, voted to you by that beneficent body in approbation of your exertions in saving from drowning the passengers of the ship '*William and Mary*,' bound from Liverpool to New Orleans.

Your disinterested conduct on this occasion has attracted very general attention, not only in England but in America and contrasting so strongly as it did with the discreditable abandonment of those passengers by the master of the '*William and Mary*,' it has reflected great honour upon yourself.

Major d'Arcy spontaneously made the representation which has elicited from the Royal National Institution (whose rewards are usually limited to shipwrecks on the coast of the United Kingdom), the Silver Medal which I am about to present to you in admiration of your humane and prompt exertions on that Society congratulate you on having been made the happy instrument, under Divine Providence, in rescuing from inevitable destruction so large a number of your fellow creatures.

... I hope that wherever an emigrant vessel, among the many which take this route, may again be unhappily, by the violence of the tempests, variable currents, or other cause be shipwrecked in the Bahamas, the misfortunes of the passengers may be promptly relieved by similar kind-hearted assistance as that which you rendered in the case of the '*William and Mary*'.

Captain Sands expressed his thanks and gratification at the communication he had received and seemed proud of the better estimation in which the wreckers are held: observing that in the performance of the services he had rendered, he acted upon feelings which arose out of sentiments early inculcated by the example of his parents.

As the first overseas recipient of this prestigious silver medal, Captain Robert Sands would go down in history for all the right reasons – unlike Captain Timothy Reirdan Stinson – and deservedly so.

Chapter Twelve

The N. York Commercial Advertiser severely condemns the captain of the barque William & Mary, now that the safety of the passengers shows that he deserted the ship, regardless of every thing but his own safety. The editor says: 'It is now plain, his report was false in reality, as it appears heartless. He did not see the William & Mary go down. He and his crew deserted their post and abandoned the multitude of passengers to their fate, while yet the ship floated and their safety might have been provided for. To cover up the unparalleled inhumanity, he made and circulated a false report, calculating the abandoned would never bear testimony against him.'

(*Wilmington Journal*, 10 June 1853)

Afterwards

Despite the overwhelming evidence of his misconduct, lies and cowardice, Captain Stinson was never to face prosecution, a trial or any kind of inquiry or inquest. There is nothing within the historical record to suggest he suffered any pangs of conscience from his treachery, total mismanagement of the shipwreck and its immediate aftermath, or the deaths of the unnamed passengers resulting from it. It is interesting to note, however, that instead of returning to sea he became a house-painter and eventually settled in Illinois, far from the coast. Wrecks were a common hazard for mariners and it was unusual for a captain to give up their career because of one, but that seems to have been the case with Timothy Stinson.

He, his wife Thankful and their four-year-old son Charles began a new life near his brother-in-law in Illinois. Thankful appears to have died in the years soon after and Stinson remarried a Canadian called Lucy before having another son, Edward, in 1861. Stinson and his older son went into business together as house-painters and in 1870 he moved to Denver, Colorado. It seems somehow fitting that he would spend the rest of his working life outside people's homes. Twenty years after the shipwreck that destroyed his reputation and his life, Stinson became active in the Central Presbyterian Church. He died of heart failure aged 71 on 24 March 1894 and is buried in Riverside Cemetery, Denver, Colorado, with his family.

Having reached the rank of captain and then rebuilt his life in another state with another career, he must have had some skills and strength of character. His total humiliation in the press over the summer of 1853 would have been painful both for him and all those associated with him. His family's exile from their home state of Maine, whether or not it was self-imposed, must have been challenging. The ship's owners, including Thankful's father, Nathaniel Purington, were also in a very difficult position. Bowdoinham was a small community, where loyalty would have been prized, especially to family members. By damning Stinson, Purington would have been adding to the pain of his daughter and grandson as well. This was not widely known in the media, though, so the owners' silence on the subject of the wreck and the aftermath struck the journalists and public as very odd.

Although descendants of survivors have spoken of the wreck as some kind of deliberate insurance scam, and these were common enough in 1860s Bahamas for the press to decry them, the fate of the *William and Mary* seems to have been the result of an accident and general incompetence rather than wilful malice. It is impossible to know for sure now, but overall, Captain Stinson's actions are similar to those of a person escaping a situation beyond their control. He told the passengers what he thought they wanted to hear, enabling him to flee by boat, perhaps gathering worthless receipts and bills rather than charts for effect and gave the journalists in New York a brief and misleading – well, blatantly untrue – statement before escaping the city. He was undoubtedly a coward and it is only because of the sheer determination and perseverance of the abandoned passengers in the face of certain death and the heroism of Captain Sands and his crew, that he did not have the deaths of 200 men, women and children on his hands.

Stinson's crew immediately dispersed and none were ever officially investigated or charged regarding their treatment of the desperate passengers attempting to gain entry to the longboat, or the brutal deaths – whether considered murder or manslaughter – at their hands and hatchet.

Stinson was not alone in abandoning a life at sea. First Mate Samuel Billings Welch seems to have become a bookbinder. Crewman John D.

Best became a grocer in Colorado and Stephen W. Perrington went on to work in a wood and coal yard in California. Many of the crew do not appear in US census records, or at least, they do not appear under their original names. However, Second Mate Loammi Ruhammi Ross went on to become a successful captain himself and several of his descendants are also merchant seamen. He died aged 82 in Androscoggin County, Maine.

Captain Robert 'Amphibian' Sands continued to salvage wrecks around the Bahamas, sometimes working as a carpenter as well, and died in 1892 aged 72. He fathered ten children and his many descendants continue to live in the Bahamas and the USA. He was a hero and is remembered as such. The now-renamed Royal National Lifeboat Institution describe the award of a silver medal to someone who wasn't a crew member or in British or Irish waters as 'extremely unusual' and 'exceptional', which seems to sum him up. As a counterpoint to the despicable actions of Captain Stinson and some of his crew, Sands and his fellow wreckers' heroism particularly stands out. They almost gave their lives for complete strangers who they had no obligation to approach in those treacherous waters, let alone save and Captain Sands' compassion for the tragic Susannah Diamond demonstrated his humanity under pressure. He deserves to be far better known than he is.

There are still many questions to be answered, such as who was killed with the hatchet and who wielded it with such desperation against their fellow traveller, what happened to widower John Diamond and how he coped with news of his wife and baby's deaths, whether the cook did indeed sneak into New Orleans using James Burke's identity and also if Peter McDonald, the cook, was black. There is mention of him being a man of colour in some accounts online, but as these appear to be a blend of fact and fiction and the sources cannot be verified I chose not to explore this within the main body of the book. Black seamen undoubtedly faced more difficulties than their white counterparts and often suffered harsher punishments and more mistreatment than the rest of the crew, certainly in 1853. It would be ridiculous to pretend otherwise and the viciousness of the cook's beating did make me wonder if race was a factor. But as none of the first-hand accounts I saw mention McDonald's colour or ethnicity – and when the authors of these accounts met black people they appear to have mentioned this facet of their appearance each time – I have insufficient evidence to be certain either way. However, I would hate to mistakenly whitewash this episode in history. If anyone has information about McDonald I would appreciate knowing more.

Of the twenty-three passengers who escaped the *William and Mary* in a longboat and travelled back to Liverpool on the *Pollux*, at least a couple succeeded in immigrating to the United States. Izaak Epkes Roorda emigrated from Friesland with his brother and settled in Marion, Iowa. He died there on 11 March 1905 aged 72. One of twelve children himself, he went on to have nine of his own. Ulbe Andries Bergsma settled in Michigan and died there aged 85 in 1912. Henry H. August, just 17 when the *William and Mary* went down, eventually emigrated from Ringwood in Hampshire, England, to Walworth, Wisconsin, becoming a farm labourer and dying there aged 65 in 1900. Ebenezer Miller started a new family in Salt Lake City, Utah and became a successful carpenter. He became a naturalized citizen of the US in Lebanon, New Hampshire, in 1868 and died in Utah aged 67 on 2 February 1894. His adopted children, so young when he left them with his parents in Dundee, appear to have remained in Scotland.

The Frisian party continued their journey but, despite or perhaps because of all they had endured, did not all stay together in one group as they had initially planned. According to the daughter of Jan Tuininga, who was emigrating with his parents and younger siblings, 'The colony finally settled fifteen miles up the Mississippi River from La Crosse, Wisconsin, at that time just a trading post in the low flat lands. They named the place New Amsterdam. But grandfather had grown weary of the bickerings, quarrelings and petty jealousies rife in the colony and would have no further association with them.' For some reason, Bonnema and his greatly-reduced party decided to settle in the region of Prairie La Crosse in Wisconsin, rather than Iowa. Their settlement and its Dutch-inspired street names is still there now.

Many of the group survived into the twentieth century, including Tiete Kooistra who died aged 91 in 1933. His brother Sake (who Americanized his name to 'Silas Coster') was not so lucky. Silas had been 12 when the ship sank and his father died in Nassau, a year older than Tiete (who became known as 'Tecter' or 'Tester') and following his mother's death in early 1862 he signed up with the 2nd Wisconsin Volunteer Infantry Regiment to fight for the North in the American Civil War. He died from wounds sustained in the Battle of Gettysburg aged 21 after a Minie ball smashed his right thighbone. Surgeons amputated his leg but he died of blood poisoning on 30 July 1863. The plain-speaking Lt. Woodhouse wrote of him, 'No braver soldier than Silas Coster ever lived or died.' Pearl Coster, who married Tecter's grandson, Roy, recently said: 'I think Silas would be happy to have his story told. I once hear[d] every person ha[s] two deaths. The first when the physical body dies and the second when the last person speaks his name.' Silas has already suffered two deaths in a way, the first when Stinson reported everyone dead and the second when he died ten years later in 1863. I hope with this book the people involved will not have the third death of being forgotten for many, many years to come.

A fair number of the emigrants who survived the wreck went on to fight in the Civil War, mainly – if not exclusively – for the North, or marry people who did so. This included Beitske 'Betsey' Graafsma who wedded Adam Gartner, a private in the Union Army and they counted Chester Cass, one of the so-called World's Tallest Men, among their many grandchildren. Irishman Phillip Fitzpatrick, originally from Athboy, Meath, served in the Illinois 8th Regiment and settled in Illinois with his wife and seven children. He sailed with his younger brother, Hugh, to join an elder brother already there and all but one of their seven siblings joined them. Dirk Stienstra, who left Friesland with his family aged nine, died in 1865 towards the end of the war. Joseph Brooks, the young Londoner emigrating with his wife, Mary Ann, also served in the Civil War, survived an epidemic of yellow fever in 1867 and became a carpenter and lumber dealer, one of the leading lumbermen in the area. His house is beautifully preserved in Navasota, Texas, where he died aged 58 in 1889.

Oepke Bonnema is now buried in Green Mound Cemetery, in the town of Holland, La Crosse, Wisconsin. He married a fellow shipwreck survivor, Ytje Stienstra, three years after the wreck, but they soon separated and he remarried Louise Spangler in 1860. He died aged 69, his colony a success.

Sjoerd Bekius, later 'Bekins', died in Ottawa, Michigan, just shy of his 77th birthday. He worked in a sawmill and married Tietje Berkenpas in 1855. They had thirteen children and Tietje grew so weary of childbearing that – according to family history – she kept their youngest son, Daniel, in her bed until he was 13 years old.

The eloquent emigrant Broer Baukes Haagsma (later 'Benjamin' or 'Bernard') had worked as an assistant medical master before emigrating, then became Bonnema's book-keeper for a while before doing similar work at Crow, McCreery and Co. and other companies. He worked for President Abraham Lincoln for a time as Dutch Consul and lived in Wisconsin, St. Louis and Illinois, before dying aged 76 in St Louis in the summer of 1907. Water claimed him in the end, his body discovered in a canal after he went missing while in a disoriented state. He was a popular man and greatly missed.

Hanne Westerhuis, later 'Henry Westerhouse', was 11 when the ship sank. His little sister, Rinske, died on board but he, his parents and his remaining three siblings settled in Holland, La Crosse, as part of the Bonnema colony. Henry served in the Civil War and was a popular man who worked with the Salvation Army in his spare time before he died in 1902 aged 60 while preventing a railway accident. A horse described as 'a big powerful animal [with] a bad reputation' was standing by the line when Henry noticed its presence and guided it away to safety, only for the horse to take fright as the train passed and trample him to death.

Susannah's family, the Stewarts, initially settled in the mining town of St. Louis and then travelled well into the Wild West, settling in Hangtown (now the more pleasantly named 'Placerville') in El Dorado County, California. Luke died aged 87 and is buried with his family in Placerville Union Cemetery under a monument inscribed with the words, 'Grand-Pa has gone to rest'. Although his first two grandchildren died on the *William and Mary*, his other daughters, Isabella, Ann and Alice, had provided more.

The survival of the over 200 passengers on board the ill-fated ship may have left the captain and crew's lives in tatters and the owners and insurers out of pocket, but it also had a far-reaching impact on American and Bahamian history. A lot of them had very large families, with over a dozen children who survived infancy and went on to produce their own considerable numbers of offspring. Many of the Frisian group were responsible for the settling of the area now known as Holland in La Crosse County, Wisconsin. Haagsma helped many of his fellow Dutchmen and women in his position as Consul, the likes of Silas Coster both saved and took lives during the American Civil War and Captain Robert Sands and his fellow wreckers drew praise and also a little money to the Bahamas.

Generally those who survived and settled in America were hopeful about their lives ahead. Although some would later discuss their previous years in their homeland with nostalgia, there was a sense of excitement about what was to come when they landed in America in the summer of 1853. For many of the immigrants, the horrendous journey had been worth it.

One of the young men on board the *William and Mary*, Hendrick Jans Kas, summed up the optimism and practicality of his fellow travellers when writing home to his parents. 'I think I will like living here. Americans eat pork three times a day and beef and that is a bright prospect for me.' It seems appropriate to end this epilogue with his words, 'Now I will stop with the pen but not with the heart.'

Appendix

Passenger List

A s often happened with shipwrecks of the time, the paperwork including the official passenger list went down with the ship. The following names have been gathered from passenger accounts, family histories, newspapers and detective work by other researchers. It is as accurate as possible after over 160 years and contains alternative spellings where found, age at the time of the shipwreck, where they came from and where they died and/or were buried. If you have further information please email me at gillhoffs@hotmail.co.uk

LIFEBOAT (made it to New York, on *Reuben Carver*)

CREW
1. ? Williams, England
2. Edward Weeks, New Brunswick, Canada
3. Henry Moore, 24, New York ?1829–
4. John D. Best, 17, Nova Scotia>Maine, became grocer, 18 February 1836–
5. Stephen W Purington/Purrington/Perrington, 22, Maine, 1831–
6. Nicholas Card, 21, Maine, became farmer, 1834–
7. Loammi Ruhammi Ross (2nd mate), 22, Maine, was farmer, became a captain, 22 August 1830–25 August 1912
8. Samuel Billings Welch (1st mate), 39, Charleston, became bookbinder, 15 March 1814–25 March 1872
9. Timothy Reirdan Stinson (captain), 32, Maine, became house painter, 1821–24 March 1894

LONGBOAT (returned to Liverpool on *Pollux*)

CREW
1. Thomas W. M. Allen, 23, Baltimore, Maryland, 1830–
2. Lemuel Preble, 37, Woolwich, Maine, 1816–93
3. Isaac M. Ridley, 21, Harpswell, Maine, 1832–
4. Joseph Roe, 21, Portugal>New York, 1832–

PASSENGERS
1. William Busby (steward), London
2. Ebenezer Miller, 26, Dundee, Scotland, 1826–94 Salt Lake City, Utah
3. Patrick Kilty/Kiltee, 25, Ireland, 1828–
4. Henry H. August, 17, farm labourer from Ringwood, Hants, England, 1 July 1835–1900 Walworth, Wisconsin
5. Patrick Cain/Cam
6. John Gannon

7. Owen Baggan
8. Thomas Flinn/Flynn (boy)
9. James Abbey
10. William Shiel/Sheil
11. Catherine McGuire
12. Bridget Higgins
13. Bridget Boyle
14. Florian Haungs/Haunga
15. German/Frisian boy
16. Izaak Epkes Roorda, 21, Dantumawoude, 1832–1905 Iowa
17. Ulbe Andries Bergsma, 26, Pingjum/Kimswerd, 1827–1912 Michigan
18. Oene Martinus Wagenaar, 35, Heerenveen, 1818–
19. John Diamond
20. Patrick Ryan
21. Rose/Rosa Ryan, 23, 1830–
22. John Welsh/Walshe
23. Elizabeth Welsh/Walshe

WILLIAM AND MARY

CREW
1. William/Patrick Ward, Philadelphia
2. Samuel P (or B) Harris, Providence, Rhode Island

PASSENGERS
1. James Sullivan, 50, 1803–
2. Johanna Sullivan, 50, 1803–
3. James Sullivan,16, 1837–
4. John Sullivan, 10, 1843–
5. Margaret Sullivan, 12, 1841–
6. Julia Sullivan, 4, 1849–
7. William Sullivan, 4, 1849–
8. Luke Stewart, 56, Northumberland, miner, 20 December 1796–6 July 1882 Placerville, California
9. Isabella Stewart, 48, Durham, 1805–
10. Susannah Diamond, 19, Northumberland, 1834–23 May 1853
11. Margaret Diamond, 1, Castle Eden Colliery, Durham 22 November 1851–3
12. Isabella Stewart, 17, Northumberland, 1836–
13. Ann Stewart, 9, Durham, 1844–
14. Alice Stewart, 7, Durham, 1846–
15. John Brown, 45, New Lanark, Scotland, 1808–
16. Jean Brown, 35, Scotland, 1818–
17. John Brown, 16, Glasgow,1837–
18. Wilson Brown, 14, Johnston, Scotland, 1839–
19. George Brown, 12, Johnston, Scotland, 1841–
20. Peter McDonald, New Orleans

21. John Dolan, 35, 1818–
22. (? Male) O'Brien, 38, Ireland, 1815–
23. Margaret Ryan, 35, 1818–
24. Mary Ryan, 12, 1841–
25. John Ryan, 10, 1843–
26. Ellen Ryan, 7, 1846–
27. Honor Gibbon, 30, 1823–
28. Bridget Gibbon, 10, 1843–
29. Judy Gibbon, 5, 1848–
30. Mary Flyn, 37, Ireland, 1816–
31. Bridget Flyn, 9, Ireland, 1844–
32. John Flyn, 7, Ireland, 1846–
33. Mary Flyn, 4, Ireland, 1849–
34. Ellen Flyn, 40, Ireland, 1813–
35. Mary Flyn, 13, Ireland, 1840–
36. Margaret Flyn, 11, Ireland, 1842–
37. Catherine Alby/Abbey, 40, 1813–
38. Alex Nicholls, 21, Ireland, 1832–
39. Mary Kelly/Kelty, 26, 1827–
40. Catherine Kelly (Kitty?), 22, Ireland, 1831–
41. W. Fitzpatrick, 23, 1830–
42. Ann Fitzpatrick, 20, 1833–
43. Phillip Fitzpatrick, 21, 1832–
44. Hugh Fitzpatrick, 20, 1833–
45. Daniel Doyle, 26, Ireland, 1827–
46. James Forrest, 24, Ireland, 1829–
47. Margaret Nowland, 25, Ireland, 1828–
48. Ellen Tobin/Forban, 17/19, Ireland, 1836/8–
49. Honora Milligan, 33, 1820–
50. Thomas Milligan, 18, 1835–
51. Mary Milligan, 8, 1845–
52. John Milligan, 5, 1848–
53. Catherine Burns, 49, Prussia>Philadelphia, 1803–75
54. Henry Burns, 15, Philadelphia, 1838–
55. Joanna/Johanna Boes/Bores/Bones/Bowly, 21, Kilkenny, Ireland, 1832–
56. Margaret Walsh, 25, Ireland, 1828–
57. Bridget Donnelly, 23, Ireland>husband in Indiana, 1830–
58. Patrick Herron, 28, Ireland, 1825–
59. Ann Martin, 18, Ireland, 1835–
60. Andrew McCluskey, Ireland
61. Mary McCluskey, 48, Ireland, 1805–
62. Patrick McCluskey, 22, Ireland, 1831–
63. May McCluskey, 18, Ireland, 1835–
64. Rosey McCluskey, 16, Ireland, 1837–
65. Bridget McCluskey, 15, Ireland, 1838–
66. Peter McCluskey, 13, Ireland, 1840–

67. Andrew McCluskey, 12, Ireland, 1841–
68. Johannes McCluskey, 12, Ireland, 1841–
69. Patrick McCluskey, 6, Ireland, 1847–
70. Sally Archer/Orchard (widow), 40, Ireland>New Orleans, 1813–
71. Thomas Archer/Orchard, 10, Ireland>New Orleans, 1843–
72. John Archer/Orchard, 8, Ireland>New Orleans, 1845–
73. ? third Archer/Orchard, child?
74. G. Morhood, 17, 1836–
75. A. Anslo, 28, 1825–
76. R. Kime, 24, 1829–
77. Randolph Soutes, 18, 1835–
78. F. Lumon, 40, 1813–
79. T. Turner, 40, 1813–
80. Dennis Callaghan, 26, 1827–
81. Edward Doherty, 26, 1827–
82. P. Ham-, 38, 1815–
83. Joseph Brooks, 22, London>Navasota, 1831–89
84. Mary Ann Brooks nee Farrer, 20, London>Navasota, 1833–1900
85. S. Farnish, 24, 1829–
86. Pat Scaby/Sealy, 21, 1832–
87. Tjipke (Chip) Durks Algra (M), 25, Barradeel, Friesland, farmhand, 1827–<1869
88. Jan Jans (John Balkstra) Balkstra (M), 29, Harlingen, Friesland, rope-maker, 1823–>1874
89. Antje van Slooten (Sloten) (F), 26, Harlingen, Friesland, 1826–>1874
90. Sjoerd Douwes Bekius (Sjoerd Bekins) (M), 23, Nieuwe Bildtzijl, Het Bildt, Friesland, sawmill worker, 1830–1907
91. Oepke Haitzes Bonnema (M), 27, Kimswerd, Wonseradeel, Friesland, 1825–95
92. Hendrikus Gerrits (Henry Ruby de Boer) de Boer (M), 29, Harlingen, Friesland, blacksmith servant, 1823–98
93. Anna Spoelstra (F), 31, Harlingen, Friesland, 1821–<1856
94. Herke Jolkes de Jong (M), 43, Herbayum, Franekeradeel, Friesland, carpenter 1809–53/4
95. Anna Aleides Voorttallen (F), 32, Leeuwarden, Friesland, maid, 1821–91
96. Dieuwke (Odelia) de Jong (F), 16, Harlingen, Friesland, 1836–1928
97. Jouke de Jong (M), 14, Harlingen, Friesland, 1839–
98. Luutske de Jong, 7, 1846 – (may have died previously in Friesland)
99. Cornelius de Jong, 7, 1846–
100. Jelle de Vries Hermanus Gersema (M), 24, Kimswerd, Wonseradeel, Friesland, minister's son, 1829–
101. Bauke (Bouk Grafsma) Douwes Graafsma (M), 38, Arum, Wonseradeel, Friesland, farmer, 1815–75
102. Klaaske (Clara/Carrie Granfield) Aukes Tichelaar (F) 29 Kimswerd, Wonseradeel Friesland 1824–1901
103. Beitske (Betsey/Bettsy Gartner) Graafsma (F), 8, Barradeel, Friesland, 1844–1922
104. Trijntje Graafsma (F), 1, Wonseradeel, Friesland, 1851–1 April 1853

105. Broer (Benjamin or Bernard) Baukes Haagsma (M), 22, Wonseradeel, Friesland, assistant medical master, school teacher, book keeper then Dutch Consul to Abraham Lincoln, 1831–1907
106. Sytske/Sietske/Sijtske Martens Hiemstra (F), 21, Sint Annaparochie, Het Bildt, Friesland, 1831–
107. Dirk Dirks Hofma (M), 27, Barradeel, Friesland, 1825–30 March 1853
108. Lijsbertus Hofstra (M), 30, Menaldumsdeel, Friesland, 1823–
109. Pietje Hollander (F), 28, Makkum, Wonseradeel, Friesland, 1824–96
110. Jan Willems Janzen (M), 23, Franekeradeel, Friesland, 1830–
111. Grietje Jans Jansonius (F), 19, Franekeradeel, Friesland, 1833–
112. Hendrik Jans Kas (M), 27, Baarderadeel, Friesland, 1825 –1880>1900
113. Jacob Sakes Kooistra (M), 45, Achlum, Franekeradeel, Friesland, carpenter's mate, 1808–6 May 1853
114. Antje Tiettes/Tjietes Piekema (F), 37, Arum, Wonseradeel, Friesland, 1816–62
115. Sake (Silas Coster) Kooistra (M), 12, Wonseradeel, Friesland, 1841–63
116. Tiete (Tecter/Tester Coster) Kooistra (M), 11, Wonseradeel, Friesland, 1842–1933
117. Sijmon (Simon Coster) Kooistra (M), 4, Wonseradeel, Friesland, 1848–67
118. Baukje Kooistra (F), 2, Wonseradeel, Friesland, 1850–12 April 1853
119. Marinus Kooistra (M), 1, Wonseradeel, Friesland, 1851–18 April 1853
120. Dirk Cornelis Kuiken (M), 24, Het Bildt, Friesland, 1829–
121. Gerrit Molenaar (M), 23, Franekeradeel, Friesland, 1829–
122. K./Cornelis Jakobs Ploegsma (M), 31, Franekeradeel, Friesland, 1822–
123. Beinze Cornelis Rienks (M), 25, Het Bildt, Friesland, 1827–1908
124. Hendrik Rienks (M), 30, Het Bildt, Friesland, 1823–
125. Pieter (Peter Salvador) Ages Salverda (M), 32, Franekeradeel, Friesland, 1821–1901
126. Maartje Pieters Schaaf (F), 22, Wonseradeel, Friesland, 1830–
127. Rients (Ralph) Sikkes Sikkema (M), 33, Barradeel, Friesland, labourer, 1820–1900/10
128. Ymkje (Emma) Sytzes Nauta (F), 32, Barradeel, Friesland, 1820–1912
129. Maaike Sikkema (F), 3, Barradeel, Friesland, 1850–29 April 1853
130. Sikke Sikkema (M), baby, Friesland, 1853–7 April 1853
131. Johannes (John) Dirks Steenstra/Stienstra (M), 38, Franekeradeel, Friesland, 1814–83
132. Riemke Heerkes Nijdam (F), 35, Franekeradeel, Friesland, 1817–73
133. Lieuwe Jans (Louis John) Steenstra (M), 16, Franekeradeel, Friesland, 1837–1919
134. Ytje Steenstra/Stienstra (F), 12, Franekeradeel, Friesland, 1840–1917
135. Dirk Steenstra/Stienstra (M), 9, Franekeradeel Friesland, 1843–65
136. Sjoerd (Shuard Chalsma) Tjallings Tjalsma (M), 43, Wommels, Hennaarderadeel, Friesland, skipper, 1810–89
137. Sjoukje (Susan Chalsma) Lykles Hoogterp (F), 40, Kimswerd, Wonseradeel, Friesland, 1812–88
138. Lyckle Tjalsma (M), 18, Wonseradeel, Friesland, 1834–18 April 1853
139. Tjalling (Charles Chalsma) Tjalsma (M), 16, Wonseradeel, Friesland, 1837–1919
140. Sjouke (Shouke Chalsma) Tjalsma (M), 14, Wonseradeel, Friesland, 1838–1924

141. Klaas (Claus Chalsma) Tjalsma (M), 11, Wonseradeel, Friesland, 1841–1910
142. Jacob (Jacob Chalsma) Tjalsma (M), 9, Wonseradeel, Friesland, 1844–91
143. Dirk (Dirk Chalsma) Tjalsma (M), 6, Wonseradeel, Friesland, 1847–1927
144. Sjoerd Tjalsma (M), 3, Wonseradeel, Friesland, 1850–26 June 1853
145. Johannes (John) Jans Tuininga (M), 40, Harlingen, Friesland, 1813–1901
146. Trijntje (Catherine) Albers de Haan (F), 39, Sexbierum, Barradeel, Friesland, 1814–98
147. Jan (John) Tuininga (M), 16, Barradeel, Friesland, 1836–97
148. Sjoukje (Susan) Tuininga (F), 12, Barradeel, Friesland, 1841–1919
149. Antje Tuininga (F), 10, Barradeel, Friesland, 1843–3 April 1853
150. Albertje Tuininga (F), 8, Barradeel, Friesland, 1845–
151. Gerrit Tuininga (M), 3, Barradeel, Friesland, 1850–30 March 1853
152. Jan Martens Vander Ploeg (M), 67, Westdongeradeel, Friesland, gardener, 1786–
153. Baukje Vander Ploeg (F), 37, Westdongeradeel, Friesland, 1815–
154. Marten van der Ploeg (M), 33, Westdongeradeel, Friesland, 1819–
155. Metje Sapes van der Ploeg (F), 22, Het Bildt, Friesland, 1831–70
156. Hendrik Spanjer (M), 35, 1817–2 April 1853
157. Petrus Jans van der Tol (M), 29, Barradeel, Friesland, 1823–11 May 1853
158. Dr Johannes Coenraads (Bart) van der Veer (M), 56, barber, saddler, vet, instrument maker, then medicus/arts, 1797–1862
159. Siebren Riekeles Wesselius (M), 56, Vrouwenparochie, Het Bildt, Friesland, 1797–
160. Marijke (Maria) Klases Hamer (F), 49, Barradeel, Friesland, 1803–
161. Eeltje Elgersma (M), 16, Friesland, 1837–1917
162. Antje Wesselius (F), 14, Barradeel, Friesland, 1838–
163. Sjoerd (George) Wesselius (M), 11, Barradeel, Friesland, 1841–1918
164. Arjen (Aaron Westerhouse) Gerrits Westerhuis (M), 38, Het Bildt, Friesland, 1815–77
165. Jeltje Jakobs Knol (F), 43, Minnertsga, Barradeel, Friesland, 1810–<1865
166. Japke (Mary Caroline Westerhouse) Westerhuis (F), 13, Barradeel, Friesland, 1839–1924
167. Hanne (Henry Westerhouse) Westerhuis (M), 11, Barradeel, Friesland, 1841–1902
168. Jakob Westerhuis (M), 9, Barradeel, Friesland, 1843–
169. Rinske Westerhuis (F), 4, Barradeel, Friesland, 1849–2 May 1853
170. Sipke (Sidney Westerhouse) Westerhuis (M), 1, Barradeel, Friesland, agent, 1852–1902
171. Dirk Siegers Zwight/Zwicht/Zwigt (M), 34, Bovenkrijpe, Schoterland, 1818–72
172. James Burke, 50, 1803–
173. ?
174. ?
175. ?
176. ?
177. ?

Acknowledgments

Writing a book about people who are long dead is difficult. Writing one using accounts mainly written in a language you don't know is nigh on impossible. I kept trying to talk myself out of pursuing the tragedy of the *William and Mary* as a book idea, to be sensible and look for a different shipwreck or other event to research and write about, but the story of Stinson and his cowardly acts towards the travellers dependent on him and his crew had taken a grip on me. Thankfully, due in no small part to the people I have met online as a result of my research, the seemingly impossible became possible, the impractical was manageable and the book is now done. Any and all mistakes are, however, my own.

Without the internet, I could not have found out what I did, contacted the people I have, or seen images from 150 years ago like the tintype of Silas Coster in his Union uniform, a curl licking up from the side of his carefully smoothed-down hair. The look in his eyes haunts me. I have had the privilege of talking to descendants of the people involved in the wreck, telling them further details of what their ancestors went through or breaking it to them that they were in a shipwreck at all. Many of the people on board went on to have large families and some, like Beitske Graafsma, would have over 200 descendants – equivalent to the *William and Mary*'s passenger list.

I am deeply grateful to many people and places for their help, support and good wishes. Although it's just my name on the cover, really there should be many, many more (although to be honest there's just no way they'd fit).

Descendants/relations
Ken Schaaf, whose book on the *William and Mary* will soon be published, I recommend seeking it out; Joan McWhirter; Kor Postma; Levi Ross IV; Kim Frank; Maggie Stern; Sally Jahnke; Kay Potter; Jewel Brooks; Moira Steven; Melinda Hill; Nancy Cooney; Ian MacDonald; Fiona Turnbull; Jayme Barschdorf; Caroline Gribbin; N. Johlsson; Jim Patete; Christopher Lindstrom; James Kooistra; John Thomsen; and Pearl Coster.

Researchers and institutions
Loren Lemmen; Colin Morgan; DP Patterson of the Wyannie Malone Museum; Betsy Steen of the Bowdoinham Historical Society; Lisa Plouffe Beauregard; Janet Sheeres; Darren White; Craig Sherwood of the ever-wonderful Warrington Museum and Art Gallery; Ian Murphy of Liverpool Museums; Keith Salvesen of rollingharbour.com; Laurie Jasinski; Sarah Bosmans of Het Scheepvaartmuseum; Jim McKeown of the National Waterways Museum; Laurie J. Mense; Paula B. Richter of the Peabody Essex Museum; Rosella Brookens and Vauna Stahl of the Christian County Genealogical Society; Richard H. Harms of the Christian Reformed Church Archives; Martin Hughes of the Scottish Maritime Museum; Medewerkers Informatiediensten & Collecties, Zeeuwse Bibliotheek; Ids de Jong of Tresoar; Amy Gregor of brightsolid Newspaper Archive Ltd.; Bill and Frederick Beseler; Barbara Leo of the Coxhoe History Group; Dee Edwards of El Dorado County Historical Museum; Alan Johnston of the

Peterborough and District Family History Society; Philip Burman; Peter Moorman of the RNLI; Anita Taylor Doering of the La Crosse Public Library; Jeff Thornton, Geoffrey Allan and Steve Palmer of the Isle of Wight Family History Society Facebook group; and Sandi Costa.

General help and fabulousness
Gloria MacLean, my ever-supportive honorary mum and maker of fantastic fryups and macaroni cheese; Diane Watt, Lynne McKerr and Heike Bauer, my very helpful aunts; Lynne Otterson, my long-suffering mum, for treating me to multiple deep-fried pizzas and chips and not minding that I kept doing research on my laptop when I was meant to be spending time with her; Pat Watt, my mega-proud Nana, who let me ramble on at length about my findings; Nick McParlin, sounding board extraordinaire; Shane Simmons and Steven 'Joanie' Wallace, senders of filthy jokes and tasty chocolate; Jennie Goloboy of Red Sofa Literary Agency, my sweet and VERY effective nonfiction agent; Coraline, Friendlycat and Echo, for ensuring that no pen, post-it, or printout was free of cat-hairs or available when I needed it (they're not *actually* meant for sleeping on, you know …); Gordon Darroch, for translation work and general advice; Mike Hoffs, for Gilly drinks and general husbandly support; Angus Hoffs, for drawing self-portraits of himself on my notes, pinching my highlighters, eating my Wispa biscuits then putting the empty packet back and the best hugs in the world ever; Eloise Hansen at Pen & Sword, who is splendid at calming the inevitable collywobbles associated with writing a book; Adrian Lea; Darren White for support, information, helpful chats, useful comments and finding the perfect cover art; Walter Giersbach; Mignon Ariel King; Curtis and Emma Jobling; Joanna Delooze; Emma Briant; Suzie Grogan; Sarah Collie; Nutella; Natalie Emma McConville; Violet Fenn; Matt Potter of Pure Slush; Mieneke van der Salm; Angela Buckley; Dr Cathryn Pearce; Dr E. Lee Spence; Deborah Cliffe of Bonhams; Warren Knowlton and his wife Judy for kindly allowing me to use the perfect painting for the cover, 'The full-rigged *Lord Ashburton* foundering in a hurricane off Grand Manan Island, New Brunswick, 19th January 1857'; David Druett of pennymead.com for generously sending me illustrations; author and mentor Jeremy Scott; @Undine; and Cheshire Cakes, for keeping body and soul together after school.

　　Extra special thanks to Colin Morgan, Loren Lemmen, DP Patterson, Betsy Steen, Janet Sheeres, Darren White, Lisa Plouffe Beauregard and every single person who got in touch after reading my last book, especially Roland Moore who made me THE best jigsaw puzzle EVER.

　　If anyone has any information, questions, or feedback then do feel free to contact me via Pen & Sword, twitter (@GillHoffs), or gillhoffs@hotmail.co.uk. The book may be out but I'd still love to know more!

Bibliography

Albury, P., *The Story of the Bahamas* (MacMillan Education Ltd., London and Oxford, 1975).

Bekins' Blue Book. The family of Sjoerd Bekius, known as Bekins in America. In commemoration of the 100th anniversary of the pioneer arrival of his wife, Tiertje Bekius (Berkompas) in America – 1847 (1947). Place of publication not identified.

Bolster, W. J., *Black Jacks: African American Seamen in the Age of Sail* (Harvard University Press, Cambridge, Massachusetts, London, England, 1997).

Brown, K., *Poxed & Scurvied: The Story of Sickness and Health at Sea* (Seaforth Publishing, Barnsley, 2011).

Coleman, T., *Passage to America* (Hutchinson, 1972). I would heartily recommend reading this if you are interested in finding out more about ordinary people's journeys and lives in general.

Craton, M., *A History of the Bahamas*, third edition (San Salvador Press, Canada, 1986).

Dana, R. H., *Two Years Before The Mast* (The Children's Press, London and Glasgow, 1840/1959). This is quite brief and an excellent resource, whatever age you are.

Haagsma, B. B., *Lotgevallen van den heer O. H. Bonnema* (P. Runia, Harlingen, 1853).

Mangan, J. J. (ed), *Robert Whyte's 1847 Famine Ship Diary: The Journey of an Irish Coffin Ship* (Mercier Press, Ireland, 1994). This is another gripping read.

Fitzgerald, P., and Lambkin, B., *Migration in Irish History, 1607–2007* (Palgrave Macmillan, Hampshire, 2008).

Hibbert, C., *The Illustrated London News: Social History of Victorian Britain* (Angus and Robertson, London, 1975).

Hunte, G., *The Bahamas* (B. T. Batsford Ltd., London and Sydney, 1975).

Lucas, H. S., *Dutch Immigrant Memoirs and Related Writings*, revised edition (Eerdmans, Grand Rapids, USA, 1997).

Paterson, M., *A Brief History of Life in Victorian Britain: A Social History of Queen Victoria's Reign* (Robinson, London, 2008).

Percival, J., *The Great Famine: Ireland's Potato Famine 1845-51* (BCA, London, 1995).

Schlesinger, M., *Saunterings In And About London* (Nathaniel Cooke, London, 1853).

Sheane, M., *Famine in the Land of Ulster* (Arthur H. Stockwell Ltd., 2008).

Snodgrass, M. E., *Settlers of the American West: The Lives of 231 Notable Pioneers* (McFarland, USA, 2015).

Websites of particular use

This pay-for-use searchable site is an excellent resource for genealogical information and meeting descendants: **Ancestry** – http://home.ancestry.co.uk/

Another pay-for-use searchable site – I wouldn't be able to write without it and I urge anyone with an interest in people, places, history or humour to have a look: **British Newspaper Archive** – www.britishnewspaperarchive.co.uk/

Newspapers and journals

Aberdeen Journal, 28 January 1852, 5 January, 1 June, 15 June 1853
Athlone Sentinel, 7 April, 11 August 1852, 1 June, 8 June 1853
Bahama Herald, 14 May, 18 June, 24 August, 14 September, 12 October 1853
Bath Chronicle and Weekly Gazette, 2 June, 16 June 1853
Bath Weekly Courier, 9 June 1853
Belfast Mercury, 14 September 1852, 20 April, 8 June 1853, 13 June, 6 September 1854
Belfast Morning News, 18 May 1868
Belfast News-Letter, 16 August 1854
Berkshire Chronicle, 4 June, 3 September 1853
Blackburn Standard, 1 June 1853
Breda Courant, 7 August 1853
Bristol Times and Mirror, 22 January 1853
Burlington Free Press, 20 May, 17 June 1853
Bury and Norwich Post, 28 April 1852
Caledonian Mercury, 3 July 1851, 2 June 1853
Cambridge Independent Press, 2 October 1852
Carlisle Patriot, 29 October 1853
Chelmsford Chronicle, 3 June 1853
Cheltenham Chronicle, 25 May 1843, 3 June, 30 September 1852
Chester Chronicle, 16 July 1853
Connaught Watchman, 1 June 1853
Cooper's Clarksburg Register, 25 May 1853
Cork Examiner, 23 March, 30 March, 8 April, 22 June, 29 June 1853
Coventry Herald, 21 January, 3 June 1853
Coventry Standard, 3 June 1853
Cumberland Pacquet, 21 December 1852
Daily Alta California, 19 June 1853
Daily Dispatch, 17 May, 18 May, 22 June, 28 June 1853
De Hollander, 29 June 1853
Derby Mercury, 1 June 1853
Derbyshire Courier, 16 October 1852, 19 March, 7 May 1853
Dublin Evening Mail, 6 October, 22 December 1852
Dublin Evening Packet and Correspondent, 25 May, 31 May, 14 June 1853
Dublin Evening Post, 24 September 1839, 9 September 1852
Dublin Medical Press, 6 July 1853
Dublin Mercantile Advertiser and Weekly Price Current, 11 June 1852, 3 June 1853, 8 September 1854
Dublin Weekly Register, 27 March 1847
Dundee Courier, 6 October 1852

Dundee, Perth and Cupar Advertiser, 12 May 1863
Eastern Times, 23 June 1853
Elgin Courier, 20 February 1852, 7 January, 17 June 1853
Empire, 6 October 1853
Enniskillen Chronicle and Erne Packet, 24 March, 2 June 1853
Essex Standard, 3 June, 2 September 1853
Farmer's Gazette and Journal of Practical Horticulture, 1 May, 8 May 1852
Fife Herald, 17 June 1852
Freeman's Journal, 6 February, 25 February, 8 April, 17 April, 22 April, 1 May, 2 June,
    5 June 1852, 31 May, 8 June 1853
Galway Mercury and Connaught Weekly Advertiser, 4 June 1853
Galway Vindicator, 1 June 1853
Glasgow Herald, 3 June, 17 June, 27 June 1853, 5 May 1854
Gloucester Journal, 10 April 1852, 9 July 1853
Grand River Times, 15 June 1853
Greenock Advertiser, 6 January 1852, 31 May, 14 June 1853
Hampshire Chronicle, 15 January, 12 March 1853
Hereford Times, 1 January, 18 June, 12 November 1853
Hertford Mercury and Reformer, 31 January, 30 October 1852
Herts Guardian, Agricultural Journal and General Advertiser, 29 January, 19 February,
    18 June 1853
Household Words, 1853
Hull Packet, 1 April 1853
Inverness Courier, 17 February, 31 March 1853
Ipswich Journal, 5 March 1853
John O'Groats Journal, 12 November 1852, 16 December 1853
Kendal Mercury, 19 February, 4 June 1853,
Kentish Gazette, 7 June 1853
Kerry Examiner and Munster General Observer, 24 May, 27 December 1853
La Crosse Tribune, 24 April 1921, 10 April 2011
Lancaster Gazette, 4 June 1853
Leeds Intelligencer, 18 June 1853
Leeds Times, 7 April 1838, 23 August 1851, 11 June, 18 June 1853
Leeuwarder Courant, 25 October 1952
Lewisburg Chronicle, 17 June 1853
Lifeboat, Volume 2, Issue 1
Limerick and Clare Examiner, 6 March, 23 June, 24 July, 28 July, 8 September, 25
    September, 19 November 1852, 5 January, 11 June, 27 July 1853
Limerick Reporter, 20 May, 3 June 1853
Lincolnshire Chronicle, 15 April, 3 June 1853
Liverpool Mercury, 11 February, 18 February, 25 February, 1 March, 4 March, 8 March,
    15 March, 25 March, 31 May, 3 June, 14 June, 5 July 1853
Lloyd's Weekly Newspaper, 30 January, 5 June 1853, 13 August 1854
London Daily News, 2 April 1852, 2 February, 14 March 1853

London Standard, 26 February, 18 April, 13 June, 2 September 1853
Manchester Times, 9 October 1852
Mountain Sentinel, 9 June 1853
Morning Chronicle, 15 January 1850, 24 November 1851, 5 January 1852
Morning Courier and Enquirer, 5 June 1853
Morning Post, 1 December 1847, 24 September 1851, 4 February, 17 September 1852, 15 January, 9 February, 30 May, 9 September 1853
Nassau Guardian, 14 May, 18 May, 4 June, 6 July, 10 August, 7 September, 2 November 1853
Never To Sail Again, Kenneth A. Schaaf, Fairmount Heritage Foundation, online
New Orleans Daily Crescent, 26 May, 4 June, 11 June, 30 June 1853
New Orleans Daily Picayune, 25 May, 30 May, 4 June, 11 June, 12 June, 14 June, 25 June, 1 July 1853
New York Daily Tribune, 17 May, 18 May, 18 June, 19 June 1853
New York Herald, 16 May, 18 May, 18 June 1853
New York Times, 18 May, 26 May, 31 May, 4 June, 20 June, 21 June, 24 June, 28 June, 5 July, 26 July 1853
Newcastle Guardian and Tyne Mercury, 26 August 1848, 20 October 1849, 27 August 1853
Newry Examiner and Louth Advertiser, 16 October 1852, 16 March, 20 April 1853
Norfolk Chronicle, 12 March, 21 May 1853
Norfolk News, 6 November 1852, 18 June 1853
North Devon Journal, 2 June 1853
North Wales Chronicle, 30 April 1852, 3 June 1853
Northern Star and Leeds General Advertiser, 1 May, 22 May, 5 June 1852
Northern Whig, 15 August 1850, 1 June 1852, 1 March, 4 June 1853
Ohio Union, 25 May 1853
Opelousas Courier, 11 June 1853
Oxford Chronicle and Reading Gazette, 23 October 1852
Portsmouth Evening News, 30 July 1889
Preston Chronicle, 18 September 1847, 4 June, 11 June 1853
Reynolds's Newspaper, 31 October 1852, 9 January, 5 June 1853
Roscommon Journal and Western Impartial Reporter, 18 May 1850
Roscommon Journal, 11 July 1835
Royal Cornwall Gazette, 19 April 1850, 8 April, 17 June, 9 September 1853
Savannah Republican, 31 May 1853
Sheboygan Nieuwsbode, 21 June, 12 July, 15 November 1853
Sheffield Independent, 16 September 1848, 4 June 1853
Sligo Champion, 20 September 1852
Spirit of Democracy, 1 June 1853
Spirit of the Times, 7 June 1853
Staffordshire Advertiser, 12 March, 11 June, 18 June, 16 July 1853
Stamford Mercury, 3 June, 17 June 1853
Stirling Observer, 17 June 1852, 16 June 1853

Sussex Advertiser, 1 January 1850, 11 January 1853

Taunton Courier and Western Advertiser, 1 June 1853

The Advocate, 4 May, 1 June 1853

The Era, 11 April 1852, 12 June, 27 November 1853, 8 January 1854

The Examiner, 11 September 1852

'The Founding of New Amsterdam in La Crosse County', Henry S. Lucas, *The Wisconsin Magazine of History*, Vol. 31 No. 1 (Sep. 1947), pp. 42–60

The Lifeboat, or Journal of the National Shipwreck Institution, 1854

The Ohio Organ of the Temperance Reform, 3 June 1853

'The Wreck of the *William and Mary*', Loren Lemmen, *Origins*, Vol XIII, No. 2 (1995)

Tralee Chronicle, 8 February 1851, 27 March 1852, 17 June 1853

Waterford Chronicle, 3 September 1831, 8 May, 13 November 1852, 1 January 1853

Waterford Mail, 5 November 1851, 24 April, 24 July 1852, 4 June 1853

Waterford News, 23 December 1853

Weekly Vindicator, 29 May 1852

Wells Journal, 21 February, 24 April, 1 May, 15 May 1852, 5 February, 2 April, 7 May, 11 June 1853

West Kent Guardian, 9 October 1852

Western Daily Press, 28 November 1859

Western Times, 10 January 1852

Westmorland Gazette, 22 January 1853

Wexford Independent, 1 September 1852, 1 June 1853

Wheeling Daily Intelligencer, 3 June 1853

Wilmington Journal, 10 June 1853

Worcester Journal, 8 July 1852

Worcestershire Chronicle and Provincial Railway Gazette, 15 December 1852

Worcestershire Chronicle, 8 June 1853

Wrecking, by Byrle Malone Patterson

York Herald, 9 October 1852

Index